The Rome Plague Diaries

Also by Matthew Kneale

FICTION
Pilgrims
Mr Foreigner
Inside Rose's Kingdom
English Passengers
Small Crimes in an Age of Abundance
When We Were Romans
Sweet Thames

NON-FICTION
An Atheist's History of Belief
Rome: A History in Seven Sackings

The Rome Plague Diaries

Lockdown Life in the Eternal City

Matthew Kneale

Atlantic Books
London

Published in hardback in Great Britain in 2021 by Atlantic Books,
an imprint of Atlantic Books Ltd.

10 9 8 7 6 5 4 3 2 1

A CIP catalogue record for this book is available from the British Library.

Hardback ISBN: 978-1-83895-301-0
E-book ISBN: 978-1-83895-302-7

All photographs copyright © Matthew Kneale

Map artwork by Jeff Edwards

Printed in Great Britain by TJ Books Limited

Atlantic Books
An imprint of Atlantic Books Ltd
Ormond House
26–27 Boswell Street
London
WC1N 3JZ

www.atlantic-books.co.uk

For Shannon, Alexander and Tatiana

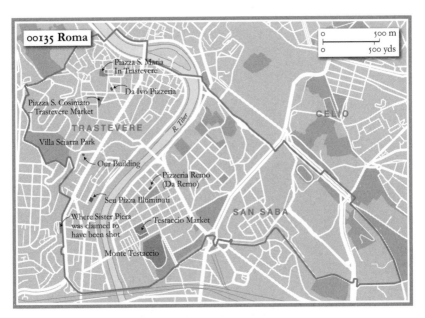

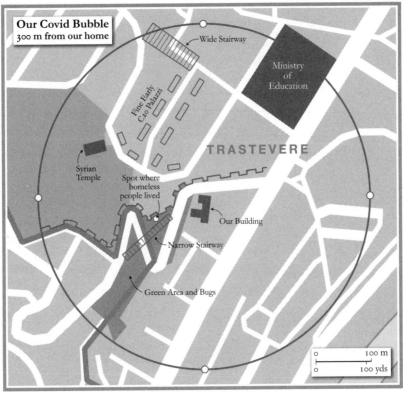

Contents

Introduction

On the first morning of Rome's Covid-19 lockdown I went out with my son, Alexander, to a coffee bar (in those early days they were still open) so we could do some work. We both had plenty to do. Alexander was preparing for his final school exams and I was revising a film script. We sat down, suitably socially distanced, and set up our laptops.

I'd been working on the script for several weeks so it should have been easy, but every time I tried to begin, my thoughts flitted away. This moment, when our lives were suddenly changed as Italy struggled against an epidemic, was so strange, so troubling and so fascinating, that I found it impossible to think about anything else. I had a strong urge to connect with far-away friends, and with people I'd been out of contact with for too long. I began writing an email, describing where I was, what was happening and what it felt like, and I sent it to everyone I could think of.

The next morning I woke up determined to get back to the script, but the same thing happened, as it did over the following days. I've never been someone who's keen on social media and is always checking for messages, but now I was constantly sending off emails and waiting for replies, and I found it hard to step away from my computer. Italy was about two weeks ahead of the UK in terms of the curve of infections and, knowing how bad the situation was in Lombardy and other parts of the north, and seeing how unfocussed the UK authorities were, I accompanied my accounts with warnings, urging people to take action themselves to reduce their risk of infection, to work from home, close offices and take their children out of school.

Some people wrote back that they found my daily reports soothing and encouraged me to carry on with them. My mother's publicist, Philippa Perry, sent some to the *Sunday Times* where they were published. When my agent, Georgia Garrett, and my editor at Atlantic Books, Will Atkinson, read them, they both felt they could work as a book: a diary of Rome's plague lockdown.

I wasn't sure at first. I was concerned that, though there would be plenty to recount in the early days when the crisis was at its height, this would change as people adjusted to their new lockdown lifestyle. But as I wrote more entries, I found they began to change into something more than a coronavirus diary. I've lived in Rome for the last eighteen years, and I also lived here in the late 1980s, so I've grown to know the city and the Romans well. I've written two novels about the city, *When We Were Romans* and *Pilgrims*, and also a non-fiction book, *Rome: A History in Seven Sackings*, but I'd never considered writing about my own experiences in the city. I didn't think anybody would be particularly interested in our lives here. But to connect what I'd learned about the city with this extraordinary, anxious moment – to reveal the Romans through the prism of the coronavirus crisis – that, I felt, would be worth writing.

This book is the result. It covers a short, intense period of time, beginning with the start of the lockdown and ending when it was first eased. I have extended the first entry to recount our lives in the weeks before the lockdown, as the virus spread in northern Italy and began to threaten Rome, but otherwise I have changed the diary entries as little as possible. I wanted them to stay just as they were at the time of writing, unspoiled by hindsight and with any misconceptions preserved intact. A time of plague is not a moment of wise reflection but a time of fear and adrenalin, of rumours and lies, of over-confidence and under-confidence, and this was what I wanted to relay.

A time of plague brings out the worst in people and the best. I have to say that when it came to the Romans – a people for whom I have great affection but few illusions – it brought out the best.

Rome, May 2020

All locked down

Ring-a-ring o' roses,
A pocket full of posies,
Atishoo, atishoo,
We're all locked down.

I'm sitting in a cafe and bakery in Testaccio, just a few minutes' walk across the river from our home. The cashier has put two flowerpots on the ground in front of her till, so you have to stretch out your arm to pay, and there's black tape on the floor to make it clearer still where you can't stand. A man wearing latex gloves comes to collect empty cups and when I go to get my second coffee, I find the staff assembled behind the cake display, engaged in a very serious-looking meeting. When the lockdown was announced last night, I imagined the Romans would bend the new rules a little, or even be downright rebellious, but no, it seems they're getting quite into this. People have an air of busy correctness, and a pride, too, in doing their part against the virus.

For the most part I feel we're reasonably well prepared. I've long had a sensitivity, even a slight paranoia, concerning plagues, probably because I owe my existence to one. In

1918 my grandfather, who was a theatre and opera critic in Berlin, married for the first time. He was fifty-one and his bride was nineteen (I make no comment). Within months she was pregnant and shortly afterwards she and her unborn baby were dead. The Spanish Flu, in mirror image to Covid-19, spared the old and was most dangerous for those in young adulthood, and especially pregnant women. Two years later, my grandfather was married again, to one of the bridesmaids from his first wedding, who was also nineteen (again I make no comment) – my grandmother.

Any word of alarming new diseases catches my sense of danger. Our friends in Rome found it very amusing when, during the 2003 SARS epidemic, they saw that I'd stockpiled pasta, cheese and long-life milk. They were right to laugh, as Italy had only four SARS cases and no deaths – and we never did drink the long-life milk. This time, though, my paranoia has proved useful. In January I usually start thinking ahead to the summer, arranging house swaps to get away from Rome's heat, but this year, as the news from China grew worse, I avoided making any plans, and put off a trip to London that I needed to make. At the end of January Italy had its first two cases of coronavirus, both in Rome – a Chinese couple on holiday from Wuhan – and the country declared a state of emergency. I began venturing out with our wheelie shopping bag and purchasing food and general supplies including, I admit, some loo paper – though not sackfuls of it. And, despite my SARS experience, I got some long-life milk.

I also tried to deal with anything that I normally might have put off. Our son, Alexander, had mislaid his identity card and I now badgered him into coming with me to the *Comune* – the city of Rome's local authority – to get him a replacement (and I'm very glad I did, as he'll now need to carry it on him whenever he goes out). When something odd happened to my eye, I didn't wait a week or two to see if it got better of its own accord, but went straight to an optometrist, who assured me it was nothing to worry about. I made an effort to buy anything that might prove tricky to get, such as a toner cartridge for our printer.

In late February a number of new coronavirus cases began to spring up in the north of Italy. This was the same moment when our children were due to go on school trips. Our sixteen-year-old, Tatiana, who departed on the Saturday, got away. Alexander, who left on the Sunday, was just about to step out the front door with his bag when he got a text to say that the Italian government had banned all such trips. We're not people who usually eat out much but over the next few days we took Alexander to several restaurants, partly to make up for his cancelled trip (he's very into good food) but also because I had a feeling that going out would soon be difficult.

By the end of that week the virus had taken firm hold across northern Italy. Though the number of cases was still relatively low, the rate of increase was alarming, and it was clear from the news elsewhere that something very serious was happening. During these same days Austria, Denmark, the Netherlands, Israel, Nigeria and the Canary Islands reported their first cases, and in every instance the sufferer was a recent arrival from northern Italy.

Yet Rome seemed strangely immune. Aside from the Chinese couple and one other case, all of whom were recovering, the city remained untouched. It seemed Lombardians were happy to fly to Africa and Israel but couldn't be bothered to take a three-hour train journey to Rome. The first new case in our region of Lazio – a woman recently arrived from Bergamo in the north – was finally announced on the last day of February.

By then we had a decision to make. In a few days' time my wife, Shannon, was set to use the winter break at the American University where she teaches – John Cabot – to go to Canada to visit her parents. It was a week-long trip that she'd arranged months earlier. The number of reported cases in Lazio was still negligible, while it looked like it would be a long time before she'd have another chance to go to Canada and her family were very much looking forward to seeing her. She decided to go. Hardly had she made up her mind when, on the 3rd of March – a week ago – the government announced that all schools in Italy were to close with immediate effect. Our children came home on the tram weighed down with every book they might need. This was Alexander's last year at school, he has his all-important final exams in May, and what would become of those now was anybody's guess. For the moment we were all in a state of bewilderment, wondering what on earth would happen next.

We socialized more than usual. We felt a need to get together and share our anxiousness and excitement with friends. We'd meet for a drink or a pizza and discuss the coronavirus; it felt somehow cathartic, as if the epidemic would be somehow tamed by being talked about. Five days ago Shannon left for Canada. Her parents were delighted to see her, though she was very concerned that she might have brought the virus to them – both are elderly and have health worries. Her journey had involved a change at Frankfurt and a woman just ahead of her in the queue for the first flight had been coughing and sneezing and looked far from well. Shannon tried to keep a distance from her parents but it was hard when they were all in the same house.

The day after she left I got together with two friends, Seth and Paul, who share my fascination with history, meeting at a Testaccio bar, L'Oasi della Birra (the Oasis of Beer). I'd imagined that, in these virus days, the place would be quiet, but it was packed and we struggled to get a table. It seemed everybody in Rome had been seized by the same mood of manic sociability. Several times the waitress leaned over us and had us move places to make way for others who had booked. In the end we hardly discussed history – we talked about Covid-19.

The next day the Italian government announced that a large part of the north of the country, including all of Lombardy, was to be locked down. And the following evening – last night – to our great surprise, it was announced that from midnight the whole of Italy would be locked down. As of today, the 11th of March, all shops and workplaces that aren't essential will be closed, and unless people need to travel for reasons of work or for medical appointments, they should stay in their postal districts. They can take exercise and walk the dog, but as far as possible they should stay at home.

Now that the initial surprise has worn off, I have to say that it seems exactly the right thing to have done. It's a great relief. Until this moment I had a sense of being beneath a great wave that was about to break, and that there was nothing I could do. Now, suddenly, there's hope. Now we can be saved from ourselves. This is the end of ignorant calculations: *there still aren't many cases – maybe this is a good time to get together with friends while we still can?* Everything is clear. We know where we are. It's not only me who feels like this, and Roman faces look more cheerful than they have done for a while.

Now, I'm at home ready to go to bed. It's so quiet outside, with no voices on the street below and hardly a car going by, let alone the blast of a car horn. It doesn't sound like Rome should at this hour. When Alexander and I walked back from the bakery this morning, the streets were largely empty. A restaurant which is normally very popular, with long queues at night, now had only one diner sitting at an outside table. He was watched over by four amused-looking waiters, all socially distanced from one another as they chatted to their solitary customer. I doubt they will have had any more today. All bars and restaurants now have to close by six.

When we got back home, Cinzia, the *portiera* (concierge) of our building, gave us the latest news. She has a kind of kiosk by the entrance to our apartment block, where she sits each morning, when she's not cleaning the stairways, watering the plants or chatting with friends. She's a strongly Roman presence in all the best ways: loud, warm and with a splendidly cynical sense of humour. She sometimes tells me Roman phrases, such as '*l'erba cattiva non muore mai*', which translates as 'The bad plant never dies', and refers to annoying people whom you can never be rid of.

She told us – not emerging from her cubicle but shouting through the glass – that there was chaos at the supermarkets this morning: long queues and people only being let in two at a time. I hope they won't have given each other the virus as they waited. I decided I'd leave the shops for a day or two, till they've had a chance to quieten down. We may yet have to resort to our long-life milk.

In the afternoon, over a cup of tea, I considered that, all in all, things could have been far worse. The weather was beautiful, a glorious early spring day with more forecast. Alexander and Tatiana were both in good spirits. Their school has been very efficient and their online lessons are coming together, so they can enjoy the sight of their teachers looking foolish as they try and cope with the tech. In some ways Zoom works better than the classroom for Tatiana, as she's a little shy and finds it easier to speak up online. We don't have masks or gloves but otherwise we're fairly well prepared. My only real regret is that I never got around to having a haircut. I wrote it down on my list of things to do and went by the barber's a couple of times but there was always a queue. Now every barber in Italy is closed. It could have been worse, as I don't have much hair left up there. It will just have to go a bit shaggy.

But then we had a new concern. Late in the afternoon Shannon rang from Canada, very upset, as she'd just learned that her flight back, booked for next Sunday, has been cancelled. News has just come in that EasyJet, Ryanair and British Airways have ended all their flights to Italy. Shannon wondered if she'd ever be able to get home. She was torn between booking a different flight for Sunday – which might also be cancelled – or trying to come home right away. Travelling immediately seemed the safer option, even though it meant she would have spent very little time with her family. A phone call later she'd managed to buy a ticket for later tonight (the small hours of the morning our time) to Rome via Frankfurt, and she ended the call to begin hurriedly packing. The last message she sent was that she was setting out on the two-hour drive to Toronto airport.

Wednesday the 11th of March

Discovering our new and smaller world: postal district 00153 Roma – and doing the virus dance

I woke to good news from Shannon, or mostly good news. She made it to Toronto Airport just in time and was now on her flight to Frankfurt, though the airline staff hadn't been able to guarantee that the Frankfurt–Rome leg would fly. What mattered was that she would be back in Europe. There are lots of flights from Frankfurt to Rome, and even if hers was cancelled, there would surely be a way for her to get home.

Concerned that I should have a good dinner ready for her, I went out on my first shopping expedition since the lockdown. There's nothing like a dose of plague to change one's sense of space. As I walked along pavements, I found myself stepping away from people coming towards me, and they did the same. This new virus dance is more difficult in supermarkets where every inch of space is filled. Modern capitalism really isn't well designed for plagues. In the smallish supermarket we often go to, I found myself awkwardly stepping by someone as we were edged close together by a huge bank of Easter eggs. When I went to pay I found that the queue – which is normally a tightly packed scrum of people – had a strangely spread-out look. Pieces of tape had been laid on the ground marked '1 metre' to separate queuers from one another, though some metres looked rather bigger than others. Staff at the tills were guarded from customers' breath by Perspex shields.

I then visited our delicatessen, Antica Caciara, which is something of a local legend. It's run by Roberto and his wife, Anna, who regularly travel round the Apennine area of Norcia – a zone famed for its cheeses and cured meats – to seek out the best traditional suppliers. They have the finest Pecorino Romano cheese in Rome and two huge wheels of it are always to be found in the front of the shop as you walk in, which fill the shop with a wonderful aroma. Roberto had put up a sign at the door saying that no more than eight customers were allowed in at any one time and had laid out strips of black and yellow tape on his floor to show how people must keep distant from one another. A Scottish friend and neighbour of ours, Carolyn, who happened to be there when I walked in, was showing Roberto and his wife Anna how famous their shop had become – a photo of it, with the black and yellow tape, had appeared this morning on the websites of both the BBC and the *Guardian*. Their Rome correspondents clearly know their food. Yet Roberto and Anna weren't too interested. They had other things to think about. They told me that, regretfully, they are going to close from Sunday for at least a couple of weeks. Operating during the lockdown was proving too hard. I suspect it will be a lot longer than two weeks.

Afterwards, Alexander and I took a stroll round the boundaries of our new, more limited, world: postal code area, 00153 Roma. It could be a great deal worse. As well as our home district of Trastevere, 00153 Roma extends across the river and includes the Aventine area, with our children's school (now closed, of course) and also the district of Testaccio, which has one of the best food markets in Rome – this was our first destination. The place was quiet and some stalls were shut, but it was still functioning and lots of food was on offer, though with new working arrangements. When I started to pick some oranges the stallholder told me, in a friendly enough way, that these could only be touched with gloves (as I had none, she chose them for me).

On our side of the river, in Trastevere, we can still walk up the Gianicolo Hill to the Villa Sciarra Park, the huge fountain where the Acqua Paola aqueduct arrives in the city, and on to Porta Settimiana in the old city wall. But no farther. Our Rome has shrunk for the foreseeable future. The Pantheon, Piazza Navona and the Campo de' Fiori, that I used to stroll by almost daily, are now foreign territory.

Shannon rang from Frankfurt where she was waiting, anxiously watching the departures board as flight after flight was cancelled. By lunchtime she had good news. Her flight was scheduled to go ahead and she was in the queue to board. I started thinking about how we should arrange things in the flat so we could social distance from one another. Aeroplanes and airports are prime places to catch diseases. For that matter I could be the danger, especially after my evening in the packed Oasis of Beer. Shannon and I share a very small study, and I moved my desk from there into a corner of the sitting room. I got out some bedding so I could sleep on the sofa.

In the early evening Shannon walked through the door. It was wonderful to see her and for us all to be reunited, but there were no hugs or kisses.

A stroll across the river

We woke to the news that Trump has banned everyone from the EU Schengen area from entering the US. I imagine more travel restrictions will follow, involving Canada and Europe. Thank goodness Shannon left when she did.

Here, the rules are growing ever tighter. What's striking about this crisis is the speed with which things change. A week ago, we were reeling from the news that our children's school had closed. The virus seemed a northern Italian problem that could hardly touch us. Under the latest decree, issued yesterday evening, all bars and restaurants in Italy, which previously could open during the day, are to be completely closed. Likewise, all stores must shut apart from pharmacies, food shops, and a few others, such as tobacconists, car and motorbike mechanics and tech repair places. In some ways, it's all beginning to feel a little Mussolini-like. A ban on all gatherings, including even dinner parties. Police checking everyone who's outside. Arrests for those who don't have a good reason to be where they are and who don't have the right piece of paper. I'm struck by how easily people have adapted. It's almost as if some part of them has been ready. And, of course, the authorities are right to do all of this. They have little choice.

There was one thing I very much wanted to do if I could: to see the centre of Rome empty of people. The regulations state that people can leave their postal districts for health appointments, to travel back to their homes and also for reasons of work. Surely the last category included me. I write about Rome, both books and journalism, and I take accompanying pictures, and if there was a moment that I should capture, in photographs and my memory, then this was it. I printed my *autodichiarazione* (self-declaration form) and filled it in, stating I was an author who needed to go around Rome for research purposes. For good measure I took a copy of the Italian translation of my latest book, to show any doubtful *carabinieri*.

I needn't have worried. When I reached the frontier of 00153 Roma – the Ponte Sisto bridge over the Tiber – there were no officials demanding to see my documents. In fact, nobody checked anything during the whole morning. Once, when I was taking a photograph of an especially striking empty scene, a police car drew to a halt just beside me, only for the policewoman inside to lean out of the car window with her phone and take a picture of the same spot. We exchanged grave looks and agreed that the situation in Rome was '*incredibile*'. I imagine the people who are likely to get into trouble – and there have been a number of arrests and fines – are those who are still behaving as if the virus isn't a problem: sitting about in groups, looking cheerful and trying to enjoy themselves. If you go around alone, keep walking and look serious you'll be left in peace. At least for now.

It was a shocking Rome I found myself in. Most shops were shuttered. More disturbing were the closed restaurants and cafes. Coffee bars are closer to the heart of Italian life than anything else. They're what pubs are to the English, if not more so, and it's hard to go more than a hundred yards down a Roman street without passing one. It felt very alien, walking and walking without the chance to stop for a quick stand-up espresso. And the city was so quiet. Not wholly deserted, but emptier than I have ever seen it – a paradise for the kind of person who stands for hours, trying to get a shot without anyone in the frame. Who was still out? Dog walkers. The occasional workman, doing repairs. A few people like me, trying to get some shots of the city. Police, and also little clusters of soldiers guarding tourist sights – though these now seemed rather redundant, as any fanatic going on the rampage these days would struggle to find victims near enough to wound.

A class of people wholly absent was beggars. Only a few days ago the city was crowded with them, as it generally is. Not for the first time I found myself thinking back to the Mussolini era. When he took power, beggars and vagrants were among the first to be driven from the streets, shunted into out-of-town slums where they couldn't spoil the image of the new, modern Fascist Italy. Today I imagine, and hope, the reason for their disappearance is more mundane: there's nobody to beg from.

All the while the weather was painfully beautiful. I could walk around in just a shirt and the trees had the first green fuzz of spring. Once or twice I caught myself thinking thoughts that I'd normally have in this season – wouldn't it be good to get away for a day or two and go and see friends in the countryside? What should we do this summer? But it's not that kind of year. It's a case of *don't look down*. Better to take on the fascinating strangeness of what's happening and hope it won't be as bad as people fear. And, most of all, keep washing your hands.

Eccentrics, and being an honorary Roman

It's getting closer. Yesterday our cleaner, Ermie, told us that a friend of hers, also a cleaner, works for somebody who has come down with the virus. Rather foolishly we didn't think to ask how close a friend this friend was, nor when Ermie had last seen her, or whether the friend had cleaned the patient's home lately. We might think twice before having her come again next week. Then, yesterday afternoon, Shannon saw an ambulance draw up outside an apartment block just up the road from us. A medic got out and began pulling on the familiar plastic suit. For the first time this is becoming something that's happening around us rather than something we just read about in the *Guardian* and *La Repubblica*.

All this does concentrate the mind. I find myself aware of days in a new way. In particular I've been counting how many have passed since I met Seth and Paul at the Oasis of Beer. It's six days so far. (Six days – it already seems like another era. We were all laughing about the virus.) The average incubation period for the coronavirus is thought to be five days. Of course, it can take a good deal longer. It's now a week since Shannon left for Canada and she flew back just two days ago. As infection rates in Canada are still low, the flight out from Rome, changing in Frankfurt, was probably riskier. Though, of course, the flight back was via Frankfurt as well.

I've also become very aware of surfaces. Door handles of any kind seem sinister and in our building I've taken to using the stairs rather than taking the lift so I don't have to open its various doors. Anything that comes into the house has an alien aura to it. I'm getting better at supermarkets. One hazard is joining the queue outside at the wrong place. Some more cautious Romans socially distance themselves so far away from the person ahead of them that you don't realize they're waiting at all, and they call out and complain at your queue-jumping. Once you finally get inside it's easy: you shop, you queue at a distance to pay and it's all done. But it's very annoying if – as I often do – you realize just after you've left that you forgot to buy the most important thing.

With so few people out, eccentrics are very visible. Rome has always had a good number of these. When we first moved here, I'd sometimes see a man who liked to walk around with an enormous cockatoo perched on his shoulder. Another cycled fast down main roads with a white cat clinging to him (it seemed to quite like it). If you walk around Testaccio you may pass a woman who takes her pet pig for walks on a lead. And now, at the very moment the coronavirus has arrived, a new eccentric has turned up: a man who goes about Trastevere bare-legged, wearing what look like animal skins. He has a pouch around his waist in which his two very small dogs sometimes sit. I managed to get a photo of him making a call from a phone box (a pretty eccentric act in itself these days).

A new eccentric in town.

*

Today has been a quiet day. Our flat has felt a little like a radio studio, with Alexander and Tatiana taking part in school lessons on their computers, while Shannon records lessons for her university. After some days of neglect, I've finally managed to put in a few hours working on the script I'm revising. It's set in Lake Chad and the protagonists have to deal with crocodiles, hippos, disease, hunger and Boko Haram. It does help to put all our present worries in context.

And the day ended well. Recently there has been a social media campaign encouraging all Italians to show they're not cast down by the virus, by going to their windows and singing something, or playing an instrument. At six this evening – the designated hour – we all duly stepped out onto the balcony and I began loudly singing something famous from an Italian opera, though I'm afraid I have no idea which opera and I knew none of the words. Various neighbours appeared at their windows, and some sang the Italian national anthem – for which they did know the words. We waved to each other, exchanged a little news with people we knew and all wished each other well. It was a great moment. I have to say, I've never been so proud to be an honorary Roman. Everyone I have come across during the last few days has been calm, efficient and has been quietly getting on with things.

And I do feel much more optimistic than I have lately. I'm sure the infection numbers will grow worse for another week or so and will look very scary, but there was a fantastic piece of news last night. In the small towns of the north of Italy, where this epidemic first broke out, and where a lockdown was first enforced, there are now *no new cases*. The lockdown has worked. And it will work here, too – it'll just take time. The Italian government is doing exactly what it should. And it's getting help. I read yesterday that medical technicians and respirators are being flown in from, of all places, China. The Chinese don't need them anymore.

If you have to be locked down, there are far worse places to do it than here. In many ways I feel very fortunate. A few months back, Alexander found a company, Pastificio Secondi, that offers a wide range of delicious pastas, delivery only, that are a little pricey but far from extortionate. We found they're still operating during the lockdown. This morning I went downstairs and a delivery man in a surgical mask gave me ravioli with red chocolate and parmesan, ravioli with parmesan and cream (we've had it before and it's delicious) and ravioli with buffalo ricotta and cedro (an obscure citrus fruit). He looked very cheerful. I'm sure Pastificio Secondi is doing a roaring trade.

Chatting with friends (at a safe social distance)

A very quiet day – I imagine we'll have quite a few of those. The lockdown has squeezed a little tighter. Today all parks were closed, to prevent people from congregating. From this evening all local transport will cease to operate at 9 p.m. each day. This, I won't miss at all, as I've had no interest in raising my chance of infection by stepping onto a tram by day or night. Most Romans clearly have the same idea, as I see the buses and trams are almost empty. But it's a shame about the parks.

Late this afternoon I went for a healthy walk. I now feel a bit bad about having broken out of 00153 Roma last Thursday. During my brief escape from the neighbourhood I didn't interact with anyone at all in the foreign zones, or touch anything except my camera, so I'm confident I didn't carry any 00153 Roma disease abroad, nor bring any microbes across the river back to us, but I feel the rules are here for a clear purpose – to protect us – and should be treated with respect. My walk today was strictly within the bounds of our zone: up the Gianicolo Hill and around. Residential streets were almost wholly deserted, with occasional dog walkers, a rare car creeping by, or an ambulance rushing past, siren blaring. The main part of Trastevere was a little busier, yet if anything it felt even more zombified. In place of the area's usual bustle everything except for a handful of shops was shuttered and the squares were empty of their usual restaurant and bar tables.

Over the last couple of days, I've run into several good friends we know in the area, and we've had the standard three-metre distant chat. In normal times this would be hard, thanks to the background din of Rome, but now it's easy, as the city is almost silent. All that's talked about, naturally, is the virus and its effects. A friend of ours, Andrew, who works in the vast UN complex by Circo Massimo, told me that the place was finally fully closed down today. Before that a skeleton staff had been kept on, including himself. He had been very glad to escape, not only from fear of infection but also because the huge building had seemed so eerie, with its endless corridors and hardly a soul there.

I talked to another friend, Liana, in front of the Education Ministry building – she stood by the road, I stood halfway up the stairs to the ministry. She told me she sometimes worried that she might be mugged when walking about the near-empty city. It's true one does feel very alone in some areas. I said she'd be quite safe if she coughed at her attacker.

A street warmed by opera

It's hard not to get a little fretful. Yesterday I woke up with a slightly sore throat, which greatly alarmed me, until I found it quickly vanished with some hot tea. When I heard Shannon coughing and coughing, I feared the worst, but it turned out she'd just watched a video on her phone that had made her laugh so much that she choked. Every cough and sneeze causes angst. Unfortunately, it's now early hay fever season so there are quite a few.

Yesterday was Sunday, and though I expected it to be much like any other lockdown day, to my surprise it really felt like a Sunday. Once again the weather was beautiful and I spent the morning on our not-quite-big-enough-to-sit-out-on balcony, working on the screenplay about the Chadians (they're having a very bad time of it, poor people: one has been eaten by a crocodile and now their boat's developed a leak). Down below I saw Romans taking walks beneath the first tree blossom, or going for cycle rides, and looking more relaxed than I've seen them of late. I suppose Sunday is still different, at least for everyone who's working online and is tied to a computer from Monday to Saturday.

In the late afternoon I left the Chadians be and went for a walk myself. It's strange how one doesn't readily notice what's absent. It was only when a small jet flew overhead – it looked like a military plane – that I realized I don't hear aircraft anymore. Our part of Rome isn't under a flight path but you sometimes hear them in the distance. There are definitely compensations for this limited existence. Spring birdsong has never sounded clearer. Nor have church bells.

The Romans are finding ways to deal with the strange silence and separation of this time. Walking down one of Trastevere's narrow, winding streets I heard loud classical music up ahead, and a little group of people had gathered, suitably dispersed. Somebody in an apartment above had a powerful hi-fi system and was blasting out the opening to a famous opera aria (if I were a better man I'd know which it was). I stopped and listened, entranced. Some people were filming the scene on their phone, though there was nothing really to see that captured the moment. When the aria finished everyone cheered and broke into applause. I felt the day had gained a little extra warmth.

We have a group of good friends here in Rome who, in normal times, meet together regularly for a drink, and last night we tried to stage an online equivalent, connecting on Zoom and chatting over a glass of wine, Shannon and I each on our own laptop to keep socially distanced.

I thought it would all be a little sad but actually it was a good thing to do. And it brought different views of what's going on. One of our friends, Barbie, who is a journalist for CNN and the *Daily Beast*, and so has justification to get around, has been in the centre of town at night and told us that it's very eerie now, with no floodlighting, so the great monuments loom out of the darkness.

By pure chance we happen to know an epidemiologist who works for the Italian health system and he says forecasts indicate the peak of the outbreak will be reached next weekend. Let's hope so. I suspect the trickiest time will be when the numbers are well down again and people begin to feel more relaxed. Romans have a habit of finding reasons to be an exception to rules. It seems a few already have. This morning I went across the river to the other side of our limited home of 00153 Roma, to shop at Testaccio market. There weren't many people about but it was still fully stocked with delicious hams and cheeses and wonderful fruit and veg – a lot is just coming into season now, including fresh peas and broad beans. But I did notice people seemed a little less careful than I've seen lately and stood closer to one another than I've grown used to. Of course, that could just be Testaccio, which is a more laid-back district than my home area of Trastevere.

I do hope people will be cautious. The more attentive they are to what's being asked of them the safer they'll be, the sooner this will be over, and the sooner we'll be able to go back into the restaurants and pizzerias to celebrate. My guess is that will be in May at the very earliest. It's going to be a strange spring.

Insanity in the UK

I fear I'm in danger of becoming one of those 'The end is nigh' people whom I saw when I was a child at public gatherings (as in this photo, taken by my father at the 1967 Oxford and Cambridge Boat Race).

But, having seen how things are over here, I find myself increasingly troubled by what's being done – or rather not being done – in other places, especially the UK.

First, a short and rather disgusting digression (squeamish people – look away). When I was a teenager I would go to public swimming pools with my school and after a while I became afflicted, unsurprisingly enough, with a verruca on my foot. I went to a local GP who inspected it carefully and then told me that the best thing to do was to leave it well alone, as it would eventually drop out of its own accord, and that afterwards I would never suffer from such a thing again. Excited by the thought of being forever immune to verrucas, I did exactly as I'd been told. After several months I began to have doubts and so walked (or rather hobbled) back to the local surgery. This time I saw a different GP, a young trainee doctor. She examined my foot in some amazement, listened to my explanation without comment but with a look of quiet disgust, and then set to work with a form of medical soldering iron. She did her work very skilfully and though I smelt a strong smell of burning I didn't feel a thing.

I have encountered a good number of British GPs over the years and though most were fantastic, selfless people who would do anything for their patients, there was a minority who seemed to regard patients as malingerers who should buck up and stop fussing. My worry is that alongside concern for the economy, and scientific analysis, there is a whiff of this same thinking in the British government's present policy. It would certainly explain the Prime Minister's statement that he had to level with people, and that many loved ones would die before their time. As for the idea of developing herd immunity, it seems a little too close to my first GP's verruca theory for my liking.

Just lately the Italian newspaper *La Repubblica* has been publishing a wealth of information on what is now known about the coronavirus outbreak in Italy. This morning's edition recounted a study of the outbreak in the town of Vo', which was among the first to be struck. It was found that between 50 per cent and 75 per cent of people in Vo' who had the virus – mostly young – never showed symptoms and never knew they'd had it. Though of course they could, and did, unwittingly pass it on. Suddenly the mystery that emerged a few weeks ago, in the UK and the States, of people developing the virus without any seeming reason, as they hadn't been abroad or in contact with anyone who had been ill, has a clear explanation. The disease was spreading invisibly in schools and universities and popping up unexpectedly among their older relatives.

Though I'm no epidemiologist, it seems only common sense that governments in virus-affected areas should close all schools straight away. Once schools are shut, they can organize online lessons and students can keep up with their studies. Both of our children are keeping up fine with their remote learning and neither seems troubled by the changed arrangements. Likewise, it makes sense for all non-essential offices to close. Even if employees are told they have the option of working from home, many will continue to come in, if only to show ambition. If they're fairly young they may feel they're not at much risk – and they're not – but they'll be putting others in danger.

The quicker a thorough lockdown is introduced, the quicker the virus will be contained and eliminated. China has shown that it can be done. As for what will happen if a government doesn't act, northern Italy offers a grim picture of the cost of herd immunity. Communities across Lombardy, Veneto and Emilia-Romagna have become places where hospitals are close to collapse. Medical staff work 24-hour shifts because they cannot be spared, they have to choose who will be given a ventilator and who will die, and they frequently become infected along with their patients. In Bergamo, a beautiful medieval city that sits just below the Alps in Lombardy, and which is not huge at around 120,000 inhabitants, fifty people have been dying each day, crematoriums are working day and night, and the list of the dead recently filled eleven pages of the local newspaper.

I continue to be hugely impressed by the efforts of the authorities here, who are doing everything they can to help and reassure. Some days ago they instructed banks to freeze all mortgage payments and announced that nobody would be penalized for late payments of utility bills. From the very first their concern has been much less about the economy and much more about saving lives.

It's an example that other governments might take note of.

Wednesday the 18th of March

On the need to connect – and a recipe for pork and slow-cooked onion pasta

Yesterday morning I was a little alarmed to see an ambulance parked outside the entrance to our block of flats. There was no sign of a driver, nor anyone else. Our *portiera*, Cinzia, wasn't in her kiosk. She's been away a lot recently, and I don't blame her. She's my age, fifty-nine, and diabetic, which puts her more at risk than most. Curious about the ambulance, I rang her, and of course she'd already heard all about it from one of our neighbours. It had come for a woman who lives on the other side of the courtyard, on stairway B (we're stairway A) and was nothing to do with the virus, but was for a longstanding stomach problem that had grown acute. Cinzia then broke into a fit of coughing and when I asked, concerned, if she had the virus, she burst out laughing. She had no fever, she told me, and had seen a doctor who'd said it was just a cold. I hope he's right.

One of Cinzia's duties is to clean the lifts and the stairways, and to show she's done this she leaves everyone's doormats propped against their doors, which reveals who's around and who's away, as those who are here put them back down again. A flat two floors below us has been empty for years. Now I've noticed a number of doors with mats propped against them. Quite a few Romans have places in the country to which they often retreat. The people above us, who own two apartments and run a bed and breakfast in one, and who are among the most organized people in the building, have gone. There's no reason for them to stay, as their bed and breakfast will be empty.

On the other side of our small landing lives an actor. When I talked to him in the lift a couple of weeks ago, he was scornful of the virus, asking if I agreed with him that it was all a lot of fuss over nothing. I said I suspected it was rather more than that. He now seems to have changed his mind. For several days we noticed a bag of rubbish was sitting outside his door. At first, we assumed he'd left Rome and had forgotten to take it down to the bins on his way out, but then we heard the faint sounds of someone moving about inside. It seems he's locked himself in for the duration. We took the rubbish down for him as it had begun to smell.

Our group of friends here in Rome had another Zoom get-together last night. The excuse was to celebrate St Patrick's Day – a good reason, no denying – and though only one of us remembered to wear green (a fetching wig) we were better organized when it came to beer and all had our glasses ready. Once again, our journalist friend, Barbie, had all the latest news. It wasn't good. The number of new cases, which had been slowing the evening before, had shot up again. The authorities have been using mobile signals to track people's movements and it seems that close to half of all Italians are still gadding about, moving outside their locality. Even now people are gathering in the piazza to chat, and there was dark talk that in Naples you can even find places open for cocktails. I suppose none of this should come as a surprise. It won't be easy to wean Italians from their sociability. It's the quality that makes their world so likeable. But they need to take a break from it right now.

However, there has been a little good news. The *haute cuisine* pasta company, Secondi, is now offering free delivery to show solidarity with Romans during the crisis. We'll certainly take them up on that. Their buffalo ricotta and cedro ravioli was delicious. And I've discovered our local wine shop, which has been closed since the lockdown began, is still open for deliveries. Not that we're short right now. Wine was one of my priorities during the period of stocking up, and we're well supplied. But if this goes on for a long time, we may need a little more.

Food definitely feels more important than ever when one is stuck indoors. Accordingly, I thought I'd end this entry with a pasta recipe. I first found it in a recipe book but it has additional suggestions from Cinzia, who often tells me about the fine things she's planning to cook for her family. The recipe book claimed it was a Genoese dish, but the father of one of Alexander's school friends, who's from Naples, told us – with some feeling – that it was actually Neapolitan. It's very easy but requires hours of slow cooking, which has the advantage of filling the house with wonderful smells.

Pork and Slow-cooked Onion Pasta

Serves four

Ingredients:

2kg red onions

100g butter

400g pork loin (if you like your meat you can put in a kilo)

2 tablespoons olive oil

1 cube of meat stock

50g juniper berries

Salt and pepper to taste

500g pasta – mezzi ziti (large, long tubes), if you can find it, are correct, though a big tube-like rigatoni works fine

1 glass dry white wine

Parsley to garnish

Parmesan (a bowlful for people to add to taste)

Method:

Chop the onions into roughly sliced rings.

Melt the butter in a large cooking pot (a heavy enamelled one works well), then throw in the pork and sear it on all sides.

Add two tablespoons of oil, the onions, a little water, the stock cube and the juniper berries.

Cook on the hob over a very low heat for at least two and a half hours. Check regularly that the onions aren't burning. If it becomes too dry, add a little water.

When cooked, the meat should be very soft. Slice it into small pieces and add salt and pepper to taste.

While the pasta cooks, add the white wine to the sauce that remains in the large cooking pot and boil down till it's not too liquid.

When the pasta is ready, mix in the sauce, add parsley as garnish and serve with a sprinkling of parmesan.

Thursday the 19th of March

Our vanished market

Every day, something new. Clearly this is no time to have a cleaner come into the house, perhaps bringing the virus, or catching it from us. We told Ermie she shouldn't come for a while, though of course we'll pay her as usual. Shannon regards this as an opportunity to educate our children in how to do laundry, how to clean the floors, bathrooms and so forth. They seem rather less excited by this than she is.

In the meantime, Shannon's personal lockdown is over. To be honest our attempts at social distancing were never very thorough. At first, she'd eat dinner at my work desk but after a while she came back to the dining table, sitting at one end while the rest of us sat at the other. It's not a large flat so we were always edging by each other. It's now nine days since she returned from Canada and that seems enough. I've happily said goodbye to sleeping on the couch.

This morning I walked over to our local market, where I've been going regularly under the lockdown, only to find that the stalls had all vanished – where they usually stand there was only empty paving. When I asked somebody in the piazza, they pointed to a piece of paper taped to the door of one of the storerooms, which listed phone numbers for all the stallholders. Just now I tried the number for the people we normally buy from, Bruno and his family. I didn't get through to Bruno himself, but to his supplier, I presume, who took my order, and we'll have our delivery of pears, Tarocco oranges, clementines, Datterini tomatoes and pomegranates on Saturday morning.

Looking back, I probably didn't need to get most of the supplies I bought before the lockdown began. I haven't noticed a shortage of anything in the shops round here, not even loo paper. I go to the supermarket almost every day, in the afternoon when there's little or no queue, to buy necessities and also to get out of the house. Of course, being stocked up will be very useful indeed if one of us comes down with the virus and we're all quarantined.

As to what's most useful to have... Hand wash, of course. From what I understand even simple hand soap is very effective in dealing with the virus. Disposable latex gloves are a good thing to have. I now wear a pair whenever I go shopping, and with them I feel safe to use the lift and feel better about picking things up from supermarket shelves. The moment I get home I chuck them away, peeling them off inside out, and then wash my hands for good measure.

We never did get any masks. I've heard bitter talk from Romans that the French and Germans kept them all for themselves, but whether that's true I have no idea. A good few Romans wear them as they go about, including some that look rather fashionable. Our local chemist's had some for a couple of days, well before the lockdown, but the price was high and I could see the chemist watching us with such an aura of greedy delight that I couldn't bring myself to buy any. And from what I've read, they aren't really needed if you're just walking about, keeping well away from people.

Last night's news told of a quite horrific increase in deaths across Italy. And yet there was also encouragement in the figures – the number of new cases has slowed. As my hopes gently grow and the lockdown becomes tighter, I find myself becoming increasingly cautious. Yesterday I washed all the glass and canned and plastic-covered items I'd brought back from the supermarket. And this morning – and I readily admit that this really is a sign of Covid madness – I washed all my loose change with detergent.

But then I'd say half the battle these days is to keep one's peace of mind, so why not?

Growing to love the green area and sometime rubbish dump below our apartment

Yesterday afternoon a large white car drove down our street with a loudspeaker blasting out the message, 'Stay in your homes, stay in your homes'. It's a warning that needs heeding urgently. Last night it was announced that deaths from the virus in Italy have exceeded the total in China.

La Repubblica had a sobering piece this morning about a 29-year-old Roman, Gabriele Mattia de Angelis, who had gone to a ski resort in the north for a few months' winter work. 'I felt invincible,' he declared in a Facebook post. Skiers at the resort included some from the first Lombard towns that were affected by the virus, and before long Gabriele developed symptoms. His posts were from his hospital bed, where he was recovering from having been extremely ill. His message to young Italians was, 'It's not true that the virus can't strike you down, make you sick, make you suffer and worse.' It's a message worth spreading around the world, as the coronavirus' best friend seems to be complacency.

As it was yet another beautiful morning – the good

weather seems never to end – and as I wanted to go outside, I tried to think how I might do so without risk to myself or anyone else. Though the parks have all been closed there is a smallish area of green just by our apartment block. It rises up the Gianicolo Hill, facing a stretch of the sixteenth-century papal city wall, and it contains a long flight of steps. At the top there is a tiny walled space with a statue of the Virgin Mary and a good view of Rome behind. The statue is basic – it looks almost as if it's made of concrete – but it still attracts small deposits of flowers.

Like other open areas of the city, and the parks, our patch of green has suffered a good deal of neglect in recent years. It's sometimes used as a dumping ground, and weeks can pass before AMA – the municipal street cleaners – pay a visit. When we first moved here the city authority, the *Comune di Roma*, had it trimmed each spring, removing the bushes and young trees that sprang up. As the 2008 recession bit, and budgets were cut, they rarely came, and the place became quite a jungle and the steps up the hills, overgrown on both sides, began to seem a little sinister at night.

A couple of homeless people set up camp in the undergrowth, creating small mounds of rubbish all around them. That they're no longer there is all down to the weather. One night about a year ago Rome was struck by a huge windstorm that blew down scores of trees, including many in our green area. I felt sorry for the homeless couple, as it must have been a terrifying experience, with branches and tree trunks crashing down through the darkness around them. The next day they had both left. The many fallen trees caught the interest of the *Comune*, their trunks were sawn up and removed, then the whole area was de-jungled and the detritus of the homeless people was removed. Though it'll certainly get wild again this spring, with nobody to come and look after the place.

Even in its worst days, I've always been very fond of our little patch of green, as it gives us more of a sense of nature than is usually possible in central Rome. Right now, there are flocks of green parrots that busily devour the blossom from the trees outside our windows, wastefully chucking away far more than they eat, and getting into furious disputes with one another, in which they kick up an immense din. They're wonderful to watch. In a few weeks' time black bees will begin to appear. They seem quite harmless but are extremely large and not very aware, and I sometimes have to dodge quickly when I see one coming straight at me. In a month or so, from our balcony we'll be able to watch *rondini* (swallows) darting about catching insects at sunset, and when they vanish for the night they'll be replaced by small bats, which sometimes fly within a foot or two of us.

At night we sometimes hear owls in the trees just outside our windows, though I've never managed to see one, for all my trying. And if I find myself climbing the steps up the hill at night – usually because I've forgotten to move the car down from the higher part of our street, where there are no buildings and cars are sometimes vandalized overnight – I often see a few fireflies floating about.

This morning I decided to have a look at what the warm weather has been bringing. I took some pictures of spring flowers and bees gathering pollen, and I was surprised to discover the small wonders that have lain beneath my nose all this time and that I'd never noticed. Thanks to the quiet, I heard the tapping of a woodpecker in the trees above me. Although, as with the owls, I failed to spot it, its presence was a revelation – I never knew we had such creatures living beside us. So perhaps this terrible virus may have a few small positives. At least it makes you stop a little and see the things that you'd normally hurry by without a glance.

All about my mother

If there's one thing I'm truly glad of, it's that the coronavirus didn't strike twelve months back. Exactly a year ago I was just beginning to realize something wasn't at all right with my mum (better known to most people as the children's writer, Judith Kerr). For most of her life she'd had stomach troubles but lately these had grown noticeably worse, intermittently causing her great pain. The specialist doctor she'd gone to insisted it was nothing serious and recommended a treatment that didn't help at all (her excellent local GP was the one who finally diagnosed her with ovarian cancer). If the coronavirus had struck last year, I would have now been worrying how I could get back to London, and journeys with my mother across the city for tests would have been even more nightmarish. Her final weeks were in May, when my sister Tacy and I would sit with her in her bedroom, talking and talking as she looked through the window at the trees, which she loved – and who knows how things will be in London this May.

Among our friends here, a good few are struggling with the chaos brought by the virus. Andrew's mother is in

British Columbia, where she recently celebrated her hundredth birthday. Last weekend she fell and broke her hip and Andrew was told she might well not survive the operation she needed. Needless to say, he had no hope of going out there. He had a very troubled weekend waiting for news, but fortunately she pulled through and within days she was back on her feet and undergoing physiotherapy. She must be a remarkably strong centenarian.

Other friends who have found their lives turned upside down by the virus are an American couple, Tara and Brian, who live across the courtyard in our apartment block, on stairway B, and are colleagues of Shannon's at the university. Brian is currently looking after his mother, who also lives in our building, but Tara went to Umbria for a week's break with their children only to find herself stuck there when the lockdown began. If Shannon hadn't left Canada when she did, who knows, she might still be there.

Rules continue to tighten. Yesterday evening the government announced that people could only exercise close to their homes, though they haven't yet specified how close. The police are becoming tougher on people who break the rules. A couple of days ago a student at Shannon's university, who was taking food to his self-quarantined sister, was stopped. Foolishly he'd forgotten his self-declaration form. He was arrested, interrogated and given a very hard time. This afternoon I went for a walk with Alexander on the Gianicolo Hill above our home and we saw some *Guardia di Finanza* police questioning several twenty-something-year-olds. We both had our documents and we were well inside our postal zone of 00153 Roma, but we still kept to the other side of the street.

Generally, we're managing well enough. The one who's most anxious about the virus is Shannon, who worries about us going out. She's also stressed because the Wi-Fi keeps failing when she's trying to record her online lessons. It's very unfair as it works fine for everyone else in the family. The rest of us have been in fairly good spirits – though Alexander had a blow today. As I've mentioned, he's extremely keen on good food and this morning he discovered that our local French bakery, which offers delicious baguettes, croissants and cakes, has closed. It's a miracle we have a French bakery at all, as all things French are generally looked upon warily in Rome. France and Italy excel at too many of the same things – cuisine, wine, culture and football – and there's a strong sense of competition, certainly from the Italian side. In the World Cup, France is to Italy what Germany is to England, if with less of a sense of dread, as Italy have no fear of playing France, whom they've beaten many times. There was a strip of yellow police tape across the French bakery's door, so they may have got in trouble for not keeping customers sufficiently apart from one another. It was always quite a scrum in there.

But it's not all bad news food-wise. This morning we had our first delivery of fruit and vegetables and, aside from a few tired-looking tomatoes, it was all excellent. And we had another consignment of luxury pasta from Secondi. Today it was ravioli with ricotta and artichokes, ravioli with organic lemon and lasagne with pistachio pesto.

Rome's plagues past

For the last few days we've heard talk that our movements are to be more limited and last night the government issued details. We'll be very limited indeed. As of today, we're only allowed outside to go to nearby food shops or to take exercise by walking round the block. I know this is the right thing to do, as otherwise the infection rate will not come down. And it has had an effect. Last Sunday I saw a good number of Romans taking the day as a holiday and going for walks or cycle rides. Today the road below was very quiet. Still, it does feel dispiriting that our bubble has become so small, and we all felt a little cast down.

I've tried to put things in perspective by reminding myself of Rome's past. After all, the city has endured plagues far worse than this one. What's more, these had a nasty habit of striking when Romans were already reeling from other disasters. In the AD 540s Rome was struck by the Justinian Plague. This was the same Bubonic Plague that wiped out between a third and a half of Europe's population eight hundred years later, when it became named, infamously, the Black Death, and it seems to have been no less lethal in the sixth century. It struck when Italy was enduring a two-decade long war between the Ostrogoths and the Byzantine Empire, and struck Rome when it was struggling to recover from a devastating, year-long siege. Over the next few years the plague returned, Rome endured further terrible sieges and for a few weeks the city became – for the only time in its long history – entirely abandoned. We have no accounts of the Justinian Plague in Rome, probably because things were so bad that no one had the peace of mind to write one, but the historian Procopius gave a chilling account of what it did in the still-great city of Constantinople:

> ...at first the deaths were a little more than the normal, then the mortality rose still higher, and afterwards the tally of dead reached five thousand each day, and again it even came to ten thousand and still more than that. Now in the beginning each man attended to the burial of the dead of his own house, and these they threw even into the tombs of others, either escaping detection or using violence; but afterwards confusion and disorder everywhere became complete. For slaves remained destitute of masters, and men who in former times were very prosperous were deprived of the service of their domestics who were either sick or dead, and many houses became completely destitute of human inhabitants.*

* Procopius of Caesarea, *The Anecdota or Secret History*, The Loeb Classic Library No. 290, trans. H. B. Dewing (1935).

When the Black Death struck, in the summer of 1348, Rome was struggling with problems of a very different kind: forty years earlier the popes had left the city and decamped to Avignon. With the river of papal gold reduced to a trickle, many Romans had moved elsewhere and disease sent Rome into further decline.

One of the very worst epidemics in Rome came almost two centuries later. 1527 was an exceptionally grim year for the city. In May its walls were stormed by a half-starved army loyal to Charles V that included a good number of fanatically anti-papal German Lutherans. Patients in the city's hospitals were slaughtered in their beds, children were hurled from the windows of orphanages, Romans by the thousand were murdered, raped, tortured and ransomed. Others were castrated, including many priests. The altar of Saint Peter's was piled with the corpses of those who'd fled there seeking sanctuary. The city was occupied for almost a year, during which time homes were ripped apart and every scrap of wood was burned in campfires. And in the midst of it all, Rome was struck by an outbreak of Bubonic Plague that, remarkably, is thought to have killed even more Romans than the city's horrific sacking.

So, all in all, things could be a great deal worse.

Last night we had another glass of wine with friends over Zoom. Our journalist friend, Barbie, told us the government is predicting that the number of virus cases will peak next week, around Thursday. I hope they're right. But Barbie also mentioned that the authorities are planning an intensive campaign of testing for the virus in our region of Lazio. She thought they may be looking for those who came down here from the contagion-hit north. The announcement of the Lombardy lockdown leaked out a few hours early and a large crowd of people rushed to flee south before it was enforced. I imagine the medical authorities are worried they'll have brought a surge in cases.

I'll be watching next week's figures with even greater interest than usual.

Making my own DIY surgical face mask

There has finally been some good news here. Last night we heard that, though the total who have died of the coronavirus in Italy had risen alarmingly once again, the number of new cases, though still terrible, was significantly smaller than the day before. Last weekend was the precise moment when our epidemiologist friend had predicted the disease would peak. Of course, we won't be sure for another few days if this is a trend or a blip.

If the national news is better, our own is rather worse. Till now the only people I personally know who have contracted the disease have been in London, two of them. Today, however, we learned that one of our closest friends here has the virus – Barbie. A few days ago, a cameraman with whom she's been working became sick and since then she's been half expecting to fall ill. Last night she had a fever and the famous dry cough, and though she hasn't yet been tested, she has no doubt that it's the coronavirus. She has quarantined herself, together with her teenaged son, and so far her symptoms are light. We're all hoping they stay that way. Her chief concern at the moment is how she can get daily necessities like milk. She lives in our postal district, if just across the river, so I've offered to take her a few provisions, which I can leave outside her closed door.

First, though, I felt I should prepare myself. I'm still not clear about government policy regarding masks, but an increasing number of people on the street are wearing them. We've ordered some from Amazon but they won't arrive for ten days. Well before the lockdown, on a morning when I'd tried to find some but without success, I went to a general supplies shop and bought some tea towels and elastic (unfortunately the only kind they had was very wide) so I could make my own.

This seemed the moment to try. I looked online and found that do-it-yourself-surgical-mask-making now has numerous sites. The good news was that my choice of tea towels as a mask material – widely ridiculed by my family – was less foolish than I'd thought. It seems that, though they are less effective against the virus than, for instance, vacuum cleaner bags, one layer of tea towel was considered 73 per cent effective against viruses (how anyone arrives at such a precise figure I have no idea) while a two-layer mask was better again. As to how the mask should be made, I found various sites in which expert stitchers offered advice, though their designs seemed so complicated that I suspected their real purpose was to show how good at sewing they were. Knowing my own limitations, I decided to opt for a simpler approach: two pieces of tea towel doubled up and sewn together. As the elastic I'd bought was too wide to fit behind my ears, it would have to go round the back of my head.

I could see a great deal of sewing was required. During my backpacking days, years ago, I had learned how to sew buttons and stitch repairs, but no more than that. We have a sewing machine, which Shannon bought during a nesting moment, soon after Alexander was born, but it's never been used. I decided to have a go. Unfortunately, the instructions were in abstruse Italian, and when I looked on the net for an English version, the only ones I could find were for quite different models. After an hour, during which I still hadn't worked out how to thread the needle, I gave up and decided it would be quicker to turn to my old backpacking sewing skills.

Then, halfway through my work, I wondered if I'd be able to visit Barbie after all. Our daughter Tatiana said she felt fluey. We tried to take her temperature with a new, digital thermometer that I had purchased for this crisis, but either it didn't work or we failed to understand it. It seemed a little mysterious. Of the four of us, Tatiana is by far the least likely to come down with Covid-19, or anything else. She is a private sort of person – out of respect for this I have tried to avoid writing much about her in these entries – and she is also the greatest homebody of our family, and is happy to spend time quietly in her room. During the last ten days she has been the calmest and the most content of us, as she's been quite pleased that she hasn't had to go anywhere. While Shannon has spent time in airports, aeroplanes and taxis, journeying from Canada to Frankfurt to Rome, and I have made daily expeditions to supermarkets, Tatiana has only left the house a couple of times, and then only when forced out for the briefest of walks. Yet she does seem poorly. For the moment she's agreed to self-quarantine away from us, just in case. As it happens this is relatively easy, as her bedroom, though it's very small, is the only one that has its own bathroom (our other bathroom is shared).

Now I was beginning to feel symptoms. My throat felt, if not sore, then irritated and phlegmish. Barbie may have to find somebody else to leave milk outside her door. At least we have plenty of provisions, while we can order more fruit and vegetables, and Secondi ravioli, too. I worked away on my surgical mask and found the sewing was soothing to the nerves. If we're all sick with the virus then I won't be wearing it outside for a long time, if at all, but that might be for the best – my son Alexander took one look at me wearing it and declared, 'Silence of the Lambs.'

Tuesday the 24th of March

Scammers – and a recipe for *Pasta cacio e pepe*

This morning our small, locked-down world seemed a much better place. Last night, as we were watching a Jeremy Brett *Sherlock Holmes* (they're very calming, we've found) Tatiana remembered that she sometimes feels fluey when her hay fever gets very bad, as it is now. My own symptoms of a dry cough waiting to happen vanished instantly, showing themselves for what they were – panic.

And the number of new cases in Italy came down again last night. So it does seem this is a trend. It's a huge relief. Last weekend I was beginning to wonder if this moment would ever come, or if Italy's measures – inevitably milder than those taken in Wuhan – weren't working. Well done to the authorities here, who saw what was needed, drastic though it was, and set about it promptly. The Italians have done it. Or rather they've begun to do it – I imagine eradicating this disease completely is going to be a slow and tricky process. Now other countries in Europe are following Italy's lead, including the UK, where, not long ago, people were being told that a quarter of a million dead Britons was an acceptable price to pay for herd immunity.

Of course, not all Italians have been angels in this crisis. Though most have followed the rules, some haven't, such as the crowds of people who dodged the lockdown in Lombardy and fled south, carrying the virus with them. More were stopped at Milan railway station only yesterday, trying to do the same thing. And there have been scammers. Scamming is a very common phenomenon here. A common ruse is for people to claim they're from a utility company and that they have a special offer to lower your bills – so special it's far too good to be true. Their purpose is to get you to give them details of your last bill so they can copy them and post you a fake that is identical in every respect except for the bank account number, so you'll be paying crooks without realizing.

In normal times hardly a day seems to go by without one of these scammers telephoning us, a hum of call centre voices in the background – taped, I suspect. It happens so regularly that I now forget my English politeness and hang up the phone. Others come to our building, as often as once a week. Why they're so persistent is hard to understand, as almost everybody must know they're fake. Real utility workers only come to read the electricity and gas meters and always give warning. And though they dress in office clothes, the scammers' utility company IDs never seem convincing, and nor does their manner, which is either too aggressive or too pleading.

Even when they do get a bite, they can be surprisingly unprepared. A few years back I was walking down the stairway and saw that a scammer whom I'd just slammed the door on had won round a woman living a couple of floors below us. I tried to warn her, though to no avail, and she seemed quite annoyed that I was interfering in the great deal she was going to get. She'd refused to let the scammer into her flat, which showed some caution, and had brought her utility bills out to him. But rather than taking pictures of them with his phone, which would have made sense, he was crouched on the floor with bills spread out all around him, copying down details with a pencil on small pieces of paper. How our neighbour found him convincing I can't imagine.

One might think that in a time of crisis such as now, scammers might leave people be, but no. Though we've had no calls or visits from fake utility company workers, it seems they've simply moved on to new opportunities offered by the virus. Just days after the epidemic took hold in northern Italy, an 81-year-old woman in Bologna unwisely opened her door to a woman claiming to be a government official, who explained she had to disinfect all the woman's banknotes against the virus. The money-cleaner was last seen hurrying down the stairway with €500.

Since then Covid-19 scams have multiplied almost as rapidly as the virus. Some are online, and numerous sites have sprung up offering guaranteed safety from the coronavirus, selling protective suits and gloves, masks, sanitisers and food supplements, all at wildly inflated prices. People have received emails that appear to be from Doctor Penelope Marchetti of the World Health Organization, Italy, which invite them to open an attachment with advice on how to avoid Covid-19 (any who do so will infect their computer with malware that steals their data).

Others have been telephoned and offered immediate vaccination against the virus if they make a contribution of €50 (a real vaccine is thought to be at least a year away). Some have been given on-the-spot fines by fake police for not wearing a mask (not an offence, at least not yet). In Palermo two men wearing yellow protective clothing, gloves and masks buzzed the entry phone of a woman in a block of flats and told her that they had come to test everyone in the building. Suspicious, she told them (falsely) that she already had coronavirus, whereupon they fled away on a motorbike.

In a time of greatly increased deliveries to people's homes, even suppliers are at risk. In Turin a delivery man was sent out with a consignment of €270-worth of cakes and ice cream, which had been ordered – apparently – for a children's party. When he arrived at the address, he found himself surrounded by a group of desperadoes. Abandoning the food, he managed to escape to his van and called the police but, although seven of the group were arrested, it was too late, and the cakes and ice cream had already been eaten.

As this seems a good day, with sick friends doing well and the number of new cases down, I thought I'd finish with another recipe. This is for one of the most popular pasta sauces in Rome: *Cacio e pepe* (meaning cheese and pepper). With only two ingredients it seems like the simplest of dishes, yet it's surprisingly hard to get right. This recipe comes with much help from our *portiera*, Cinzia, and also Anna, the wife of Roberto – the owners of our legendary local delicatessen – and follows numerous failed attempts of my own, in which I ended up with a soupy, clumped up mess.

Cacio e pepe

Serves four

Ingredients:

300g Pecorino Romano cheese – any will do, but if it's medium aged, better still

Whole black peppercorns – a good amount, depending how hot you want it

500g pasta – spaghetti is commonly used, but it also works well with a large tube pasta, such as rigatoni

Method:

Begin heating a pan of water for the pasta.

Grate the pecorino cheese as finely as your grater will manage. Make sure there are no lumps or shavings as these will clump.

Crush the peppercorns fairly finely.

Begin cooking the pasta.

Take out several ladlefuls of water from the pasta pot and set aside till it's cooled enough to touch with your finger.

Put two thirds of the grated pecorino in a large serving bowl, add the lukewarm water little by little, mixing with a whisk, till you have a smooth, thick cream.

Add the black pepper to the cream.

When the pasta is al dente, drain and, after letting it cool for a second or two, pour it into the bowl with the cream and mix thoroughly. Sprinkle more pecorino cheese on top and serve at once.

For variety, you can add white pepper to the black and, for a more tangy version, the grated zest of a lemon or two. If you can find them, the recipe is also very good with courgette flowers. Remove the stamens, dab the petals lightly with olive oil and bake them in the oven for three minutes. When you're mixing the pasta and the pecorino cream, throw in the courgette flowers.

About our building

Things are continuing to look up a little. The number of new cases in Italy fell again last night, which makes three days in a row. Our friend Barbie, who has the virus, is doing well, which is great news. Last night I contacted our *portiera*, Cinzia, whom I've also been worried about, as when last heard from she had a bad cough, but she's fine too. She said she'll be back at work on Saturday, and though I urged her to stay away, as she's diabetic and so at risk, her doctor has only given her time off until then. I still don't understand who's supposed to be at work and who is not. There are so few people driving or using the buses and trams that I assume most are at home. It seems unfair to make a diabetic *portiera* venture out.

Now that things are settling down a little, this seems a good moment to say something about the place where we spend almost every sleeping and waking hour – our apartment block. It has sixty-two flats and in plan it resembles a misshapen 'U'. Like many Rome buildings it's orange in colour, though it hasn't been painted for thirty years and is quite faded. It was built in either 1918 or 1920, I've never been able to establish which, though I rather hope it was 1920. This is because the floors are supported by a curious arrangement of metal beams, which are on the flexible side, and in the larger rooms you can feel them bounce slightly under your feet. I'd prefer to think we're supported by 1920 metal, as in 1918 I imagine every ounce of decent steel was being used to make guns and shells.

At the end of our street is the Viale Trastevere, where trams still rumble by, though now only till 9 p.m. In the other direction is our green area, lodged beneath a stretch of the city's papal wall that snakes up the Gianicolo Hill. It was built half a century after Rome's terrible sacking of 1527, in a grand example of shutting the stable door after the horse has bolted. Italy's renowned patriot and freedom fighter, Giuseppe Garibaldi, was the only one who made any use of it when, in 1849, he valiantly defended the city for several weeks against a huge French army, and the hill above us became a vast battlefield.

At the base of the wall just opposite our flat, there's what looks like a tunnel entrance, closed off by locked metal gates. I thought it a little mysterious until, soon after we first moved into our flat, twelve years ago, a glassmaker came to fit an internal window in a bathroom. He told us, excitedly, that he'd lived in our building as a child, and that the tunnel was the entrance to an old air raid shelter. He'd gone down there himself with his family during the last war, listening anxiously as Allied bombs rained down.

Some fell very near, as one can see from the presence of incongruously modern buildings in our neighbourhood, which sprang up from bomb sites. The papal wall itself has a few dangers. A section at the top of the hill collapsed forty years ago and is still fenced off. Trees that grow near the wall can be unstable, as their roots are blocked by its foundations and can only grow in one direction. Occasionally one will topple over without warning, crushing cars.

Romans are very security conscious and our building has several layers of protection. First, facing the street, there is a high and very sturdy metal gate, which would be very effective against marauders except that it's usually left wide open. Next, just inside the gate on the left, we're guarded by Cinzia, sitting in her kiosk – at least in the mornings, which is when she works, and when she's not off having a coffee or chatting with friends. Cinzia does her best to keep the building looking good. She has covered the walls of her kiosk with all kinds of pictures and above it, for twelve months a year, a pair of snowmen wish everybody '*Buon Natale*'. She waters the pot plants in our courtyard, though there's not much beautification to be done there. Most Roman apartment blocks have a feature or two to offer a sense of grandeur, but our courtyard has only a bike rack – agreed on after years of condominium arguing – along with an arrangement which, from a distance, looks faintly like a fountain, but is in fact a large bowl with a plaster cherub perched in the middle.

The courtyard of our apartment block.

The third line of protection is the most effective. Each of the three stairways has its own sturdy gate, and these are usually kept closed. On our stairway – A – the building is wider and the flats less cramped, and we also have the least tiny lift. This is a rather beautiful wooden device, that dates from the Mussolini years and still has a sign written in distinctive Fascist-era lettering warning one not to bang the doors. When we first moved in, the wood panelling inside the lift was scratched with ancient graffiti, and that most Roman of emblems, a penis and balls, but it has since been cleaned up.

Among the building's inhabitants are several family dynasties, who have been here for almost as long as it has existed, and who each own several flats. From what we've heard, there was once a tradition of marrying across the courtyard. Teenagers would observe each other through the slats of their shutters, then chat down below, and end up at the altar.

Like many in Rome, our building has a few ancient disputes between neighbours. These are brought out for airing at the condominium meetings, which are held every few months and which I rather dread. A few of our neighbours are practised shouters, while the meetings are held in a basement room attached to a nearby Renaissance church, whose acoustics seem designed to funnel every decibel straight into one's ears. But I feel I have to go, as someone in the building sometimes puts down an anonymous motion to have Cinzia dismissed. I stand up and do my best, in my bad Italian, to defend her, and – no thanks to me, I'm sure – the motions are always easily dismissed. If she has an enemy or two, she has far more friends.

And, like any self-respecting Rome apartment block, we have an ongoing legal tussle. This is between the condominium and members of one of the building's old dynasties, who live at the very top of stairway A, on the other side of the lift shaft from us. This family has made various changes to their flat and the terrace beside it, and the condominium is accusing them of abusive construction (I'll say no more for fear of being sued myself). The dispute has been going on for years and shows no sign of ending any time soon.

I'm very fond of most of our neighbours. They're generally friendly and if I pass one of them in the area, they'll always wave and say hello. Most are responsible people who want our building well cared for. When we arrived, we were the only *stranieri* (foreigners) here, but this is no longer the case. As well as the American couple, Tara and Brian, we now have Carolyn, who is an artist from Scotland, and her husband, Jim, who is Finnish and works for the UN. We'd known them a little for years – the foreigner community in Rome is a village – but now that they're neighbours we've become good friends. Recently we've started having long-distance drinks with them, as they sit by their window and we sit on our balcony, talking via our mobile phones on speaker.

Finally, like any good Roman apartment block, we have a large number of elderly people. These I no longer see at all. I assume they've either been whisked away from Rome by their families, or are lying low in their homes, waiting for all of this to end. And very wise they are, too.

How to buy a used car in Rome

This morning we had a small adventure, at least by the standard of these times. Six months ago, we arranged an appointment for our children to have vaccinations. I'd assumed these would be cancelled because of the coronavirus but when I contacted the vaccination centre, they said we could still come in as the next available slot would be many months away, too late for the sequence of jabs to be completed. After years of budget cuts, it's hard to arrange vaccinations here.

I began preparing for our most challenging expedition since the lockdown began. By chance our local chemist had some masks on sale yesterday, and though they seemed overpriced, at €12.50 each, Shannon bought four. We already had rubber gloves as I'd found some in a supermarket a week or so ago. I set to work on all our *autodichiarazione* forms. The government has recently updated these, and they now require so much information and take so long to fill out that anyone would think twice about stepping outside their door (clearly the intention). I made sure every detail was correct as I didn't want to take any chances. The punishment for being outside without valid reason is now a €500 fine and a criminal record. What was more, I'd decided to drive to the vaccination centre, and if there was any car that the police were sure to flag down, it was ours.

It's hard to believe that it once looked almost new, but it did. We got it after its predecessor died abruptly on a motorway in Puglia, and the process of buying it was quite an education for me. Dents and scrapes are to Roman cars what scars are to duellists, so I saw no point in buying a new one, even if we could have afforded such a thing. I picked a make and model that seemed right for us and began scouring the Italian second-hand car website, subito.it. I'd been warned to be careful, as it's easy to unwittingly buy a stolen vehicle, and when I found one for sale with lowish mileage and a fair price, I was reassured to see that it was being sold by a dealership that looked well established. The website had a photograph of a showroom and a dealer shaking hands with a smiling girl, standing in front of an Alfa Romeo convertible.

When I went in search of the place, however, I walked by it three times before I saw it, as it wasn't a showroom but a small shed, containing little more than a desk and the dealer's rusty motorbike. How the dealer, the girl, the photographer and an Alfa Romeo had all been squeezed inside at one time I couldn't imagine. It was the kind of operation that could vanish in an hour. The car we were purchasing wasn't even parked outside but a mile away – we were given a lift by a friend of the dealer – in an underground car park where several dubious-looking types stood about, watching.

As I test-drove the car, I wondered what to do. I needed a car right away, to drive our children to school each morning, and I didn't want to begin the whole searching process all over again, yet I had no wish to do anything illicit. It was, I suspect, a very Roman dilemma. Legal process here can be achingly slow and convoluted, forcing people to rely on snap judgements of trust. Romans try to lessen risks by dealing as far as possible with people well known to them, but that's not always possible.

In the end I did what I imagine most Romans would do. I forgot about the shed showroom and the car – which drove fine – and concentrated on the dealer. What swayed me was his bureaucratic carefulness. When we'd first arrived he photocopied and carefully checked my documents and then fussed over an insurance policy that covered me during the test drive. A cheat would never have been so meticulous – he would just have wanted my money as quickly as possible. What impressed me most of all, though, was that I could see he was trying to decide if he trusted *me*. His risk was smaller than mine – time on paperwork wasted if he never heard from me again – but it was still a risk.

I agreed the sale and everything turned out fine. That was seven years ago. Our car is now a young teenager and has acquired a good number of Roman dents and scrapes.

It suffered badly one very hot summer, when stickiness from the trees above became fused onto the paintwork, producing a mottled effect. We hardly use it now, as our children both go to school by tram, and we rarely remember to have it cleaned. A few weeks ago someone rather unkindly scratched '270€' on the bonnet, though to be honest I'm not sure it's worth even that.

In the end no police flagged us down on our way to the vaccination centre, where everything passed off smoothly. The medical staff weren't very good at keeping social distance, but then Romans, I've noticed, really aren't. In the supermarkets they often forget and brush past you, especially if they're talking on their phones. It's not surprising. Romans stand closer to each other than people in northern countries, and they connect more. Systems and rules work as best they can, but deep down what matters here is personal interaction. During this epidemic I imagine the consequences of this will be both good and bad. Bad because it will be harder to prevent people from infecting one another. Good because people will be less likely to be ignored or forgotten. Romans keep an eye out for each other.

Roman love of regularity, homeless Romans and Romani Romans

Walking round the block, going to the supermarket and back, I still find it hard to get used to the shuttered shops. The streets seem all the emptier because this is a city where you expect to come across people you know, or at least recognize. Rome is the opposite of London, where people descend into Tube stations assuming they won't meet anybody familiar to them, and are taken aback if they do.

Of course, Rome is much smaller than London and, as a Mediterranean city, its inhabitants connect more easily with one another. But another reason it can seem so village-like, I suspect, is that it's a place of regular habits. Many Romans like it that way. I once got into a fixed routine of taking our children to school and then walking to a small park on the Gianicolo Hill, where the view of the city was particularly fine, and I'd sit on a bench and work, writing longhand. Once a perfect stranger came up and told me, 'Here you are again, right on time. I could set my watch by you.' It was said with great approval.

Rome can be remarkably unchanging. If you search out

a bar or restaurant that you haven't visited for fifteen years, there's a good chance that, not only will it still exist, but most of the people working there will be the same. Years ago, we often went to a restaurant in the ghetto called Sora Margherita: a tiny two-room place, which had a very short menu including delicious Jewish-style deep-fried artichokes – you pull off the leaves and eat them like crisps – and the tastiest *agnolotti* (a pasta stuffed with meat) that I've ever had, handmade and roughly shaped. One day we were sorry to discover it had closed down. A few years later I happened to be passing nearby and thought I'd go and see if another restaurant had opened in its place. There, to my surprise, was Sora Margherita, brought back to life after years of closure. The waiter had changed but not the name, the short menu, nor even the prices. The *agnolotti* and Jewish artichoke tasted precisely the same as they always had. I can't imagine such a thing happening anywhere else but here.

It's not only bars and restaurants that can have a strong sense of regularity. Even the city's beggars do. These people have been a feature of Rome's streets for so long they're a part of the city's soul, though, unsurprisingly, they're rarely welcomed, and on a number of occasions the authorities have tried to be wholly rid of them. During the cold centuries of the Little Ice Age, which occurred during the Renaissance and Baroque eras and blighted Europe with bad harvests, so many desperate people descended on Rome that the popes built a vast poor house on the Trastevere riverside – San Michele – where beggars were housed in jail-like cells and were to be transformed into hard-working citizens (the building is still there and now contains libraries and state archives). Though San Michele did nothing to reduce the number of the city's homeless, it grew to become one of the finest colleges in the city, where orphans were taught a wide variety of trades and, if they showed an aptitude for art, they were tutored by Rome's best painters. Standards were so high that the wealthy paid for their children to study there and to live alongside the poorest Romans in their cells.

Mussolini had a simpler approach to the problem of beggars. To stop them spoiling the shine of his new, modern, Fascist capital, he had them arrested and deported to out-of-town slums which were so badly connected by public transport that they found it very hard to return. Of course, when his regime collapsed everything quickly returned to how it had always been.

These days Rome has three main groups who will call out to you asking for change. The most recent arrivals are from Africa and Asia and have made the dangerous sea-crossing to Sicily. The most ancient group, who have been here for millennia, are the Italian homeless, whose numbers have greatly swelled since the 2008 financial crash. Like Travellers in the UK, many of them are now accompanied by dogs. Finally, there are the Romani people (once known as Gypsies). Though some have been in Rome for several centuries, most have been coming from Eastern Europe since the 1970s, and they live in encampments around the edge of the city, where conditions are scandalously poor. All three groups are regarded by some Romans with weary annoyance, though others treat them with conspicuous kindness.

The Italians with dogs and the African arrivals rarely stay in the same place for long, but the Romani people are remarkably fixed in their ways. If I go for a walk around the city, I see people sitting in the same spots that they occupied when we first moved here, eighteen years ago. In all that time I've generally exchanged few words with them, beyond wishing them good morning as I hand over fifty centesimi (how can you not when you've been asked for eighteen years?), yet I feel I somehow know them well.

There's a large, baffled-looking man who points at a big dent in his forehead to show why he's in need. It looks like he was injured by machinery or kicked by a horse. Early in the morning he's brought to his post outside our nearest bar by a small, sharp-eyed woman, who comes back later to collect him. I always assumed she was his wife, till I heard her angrily denying this to someone who'd made the same mistake. She seemed most affronted.

There's the old man who sits in the lane that leads into our main square in Trastevere, Piazza Santa Maria, who plays the accordion and who always seems in the best of moods, so the sight of him lifts one's spirits. Whether he finds this helps him in his work or it's just his nature, I couldn't say, but there's nobody more cheerful-looking in the neighbourhood.

By our local market there's a man who looks so serious and authoritative that one could imagine him on television reading the news. He's evidently aware that he doesn't have the right sort of face for begging and occasionally, when a good number of tourists are about who don't know him, he feigns a bad leg. His son, who begs in the same area, makes no secret of the fact that he is gay. Romans are not without prejudice, and Roman marketeers are less reformed than most, yet he seems well liked in our market, and I've noticed Bruno's daughter, Sara, and her boyfriend, Matteo, let him leave possessions at their stall and will often give him a bite of something to eat.

There's a man with wild eyes and a long beard who used to have a spot on the other side of the city centre, on a short flight of stairs near the Terrazza del Pincio. Here he would quietly moan and wail as if he wasn't right in the head. Discouraged by his biblical appearance, I didn't give him money (I can't give to everyone as there are too many) and after a time I realized that, when I walked by him, his moan would change to a drawn out and almost imperceptible 'Fanculo' (Fuck you). He's now moved to the Ponte Sisto, not far from us, and has given up moaning. I give him a coin when I go by and we sometimes have a short chat. His name is Simeone, he's from the town of Sibiu in Romania, and he seems a decent man, though you can see in his eyes that he's had an extremely tough life. I'm sure they all have.

And now it will be even tougher. They'll be trying to get through the days in their encampments. Last year when the right-wing populist Matteo Salvini of the Lega party was interior minister, he closed some of these down, in a move that would have made Mussolini proud, but I understand they've now come back to life. How their inhabitants can survive at the moment without begging for money is hard to comprehend. Nor can it be easy for them to constantly wash their hands and maintain social distance with next to no amenities.

These things will be harder again for Rome's estimated 8,000 homeless people. I've heard that a small tent city of them has grown up not far from our home, on the Tiber embankment (I can't go and check as it's outside our new bubble). They can get a meal three days a week from a soup kitchen at the church association of Sant'Egidio, not far from us in Trastevere, and box meals on other days. A few sleep out in the streets near our apartment and they look lost and scared. At a time when the police are patrolling the city to make sure everyone stays at home, what do you do if you don't have one?

Rome: the city that globalization forgot

This morning, as promised, Cinzia came to work. She looked a little anxious, as well she may, but it was very good to see her. She told me of the wonderful dinners she's been making for her family. She's even baked her own bread. She also confirmed that our building has had no cases of the virus so far, which is good to know.

And we had another delivery of fruit and vegetables, this time brought by Bruno's daughter, Sara, and her boyfriend, Matteo. They were very careful to keep their distance, leaving all five bags on the ground for me to take, and giving me my change with the longest arm-reach possible. I finally cleared up the mystery of why, when I rang last time, I got through to someone I didn't know. It turns out there are two Brunos in our market and I'd rung the wrong one. I'd thought he looked a little shifty when he delivered the groceries to us – and some of the tomatoes were wrinkled. He'd have kept the good ones for his real customers.

Thanks to Sara and Matteo, if we fall sick and have to self-isolate we could last for several weeks. We'd only need outside help for fresh milk and bread. In the end our friend

Barbie, who's still quarantined, chose to be supplied by her ex-partner, Andrew (they separated some years ago but have managed to keep on good terms). I ran into Andrew this afternoon on my way back from the supermarket, and he told me he goes to her flat every other day to leave bags of supplies outside her closed door. When he walks there, weighed down with bags, everything's fine, but when he comes back over the bridge – bagless – people sometimes call out from passing cars, angrily asking what he thinks he's doing. But then, Andrew does seem unlucky when it comes to attracting Covid disapproval. A few mornings ago he was standing in a deserted, marketless Piazza San Cosimato, sending a text and enjoying a moment outside his nearby flat, when he became aware of a loud whirring of helicopter rotor blades just above him. A moment later a voice called out, '*A casa!*' (Go home!). It was the police. Andrew went home, and quickly.

There's nothing like a plague to change one's view of your local supermarkets. We have six that are near enough to satisfy the latest rules. Compared to the giants one finds in North America and northern Europe, they're all very small, yet they're surprisingly diverse and most have their own specialization. The tiniest of them, which is hardly bigger than a mini-mart, has the best fruit and vegetables. Another, just beside it, doubles as a butcher and prepares its own good-quality meat. A third, which is the largest in our area, and which we go to fairly often in ordinary times, has an excellent fresh fish counter and a tank of live lobsters. A fourth offers cheapness. We normally avoid it, as the brands are poor and it's on a rather sinister street, but now it has become our local. It's so unpopular and empty that you never need to queue and there's less chance of someone brushing past you as they chatter on their phone.

I've heard Rome described as 'the city that globalization forgot' and there's a good deal of truth in this. While much of the world is filled with chains, here most shops, bars and restaurants are still one-offs. One of our local supermarkets is staffed by an extended family. The first Starbucks in Rome was to open in January, near the Vatican, but has run into trouble with paperwork and now Covid. McDonald's has been more successful and the chain has no fewer than forty restaurants in Rome, mostly in the suburbs (a proposal for a huge new one by the Terme di Caracalla [the Baths of Caracalla] was recently thwarted by the country's minister of culture), but even these can be subverted. One day when Shannon was pregnant with Alexander and we were driving outside Rome, she felt a need for the comfort of junk food; we stopped at one and were surprised to see that, as well as the usual offerings of burgers and fries, there was a shelf of delicious-looking homemade cakes. I'm sure these contravened every one of the burger chain's directives, but there they were.

These days the Roman way of doing things is proving very useful. In recent days British and North American supermarkets have been emptied by panic buyers and, thanks to their financially efficient *just in time* supply lines, restocking has proved a considerable problem, as the system is designed to be so taut that there's no flexibility. Italy has had empty shelves too, of course (though I never saw any in our neighbourhood, even for loo paper), but here improvisation is easier because links are more personal. As in the case of Sara and Matteo bringing delicious tomatoes and oranges and aubergines from the fields of Latina direct to our door.

A bad day at the supermarket, and getting to know our new bubble

This virus sends you up and down like a yo-yo, and today was down. An old friend of ours, Yvonne, who was once our neighbour in Rome and who has now moved back to her native Holland, almost certainly has the virus. She has three school-age children, has serious underlying health problems, and her husband – who is a heart surgeon – is stuck in Albania. He works there and the Albanian authorities, understandably, don't want to lose any medical staff. Yvonne's messages sound scared. It's hard because there's nothing we can do except stay in contact, and tell her all our thoughts are with her.

If that's not bad enough, there are also the figures. It's hard not to fixate on them, and check the moment the latest are announced, each evening at six. They read like a kind of terrible, inverted Olympic Games medal table. For silver: new cases. For gold: new deaths. I scan the lists, hoping my adopted country has won fewer this time. Yet what do these figures really mean? We're told the curve of new cases is slowing but how reliable is this information? There's no doubt that our journalist friend, Barbie, has had the virus, as she's had a fever and the telltale cough, and she rang the health number to inform them, but she was never tested – happily her condition hasn't become sufficiently serious – so she hasn't been added to the list.

The one figure that's absolutely certain is deaths. Of course this number doesn't reflect contagion rates now, but rather several weeks ago, when the newly dead of today were first infected. For days afterwards they would have continued to shop and walk the dog, ignorant that the virus was multiplying inside them. When they first developed a fever and cough their symptoms would have been mild for a time and they would have hoped that they would quickly pass. Till the moment came when they found it hard to breathe and rang for an ambulance, and then took their place at the local hospital, where the virus overwhelmed their body's defences and they became added to the official tally. Yet, even if we're viewing the past rather than the present, that doesn't lessen the alarming scale of what's going on. Coronavirus deaths in Italy have now passed 10,000 people. China's deaths all but halted at a third of that number. Italy is far ahead of any other country in gold medals at the Coronavirus Olympics.

With all of this alarming information buzzing in my head, I went to the supermarket. We're well stocked up on food yet somehow it seems we always need something more. We are bad at planning ahead. At lunchtime we decide what to have for dinner, we choose something that's complicated to cheer everybody up, and of course we don't have all the right ingredients. And we always need milk. I buy four litres at a time, but the more I get the more quickly it's drunk, mostly by my children. It must be a comfort thing.

I went to the supermarket that's run by the family dynasty, as they're the most careful to try and keep people apart from one another at the tills. But of course, that doesn't mean they can control their customers elsewhere in the shop. An old man just ahead of me stopped and began addressing a seemingly endless series of questions to the daughter of the dynasty, who was restocking a fridge. They were beside the huge display of Easter eggs that presses out into the aisle, making it impossible to get by. I felt my impatience rising. Do we even need Easter eggs? Are we still doing Easter? I suppose you can't *not* do it. Then a man with no mask and no sense of caution, who had been ahead of me before but had then vanished, suddenly sprang out from a niche full of wine and pushed right in front of me, breathing right in my face. Now we were both caught behind the old man. 'And where's the flour? I don't understand. Is that by the fridge with the fresh pasta? No? Then which one?' Someone was right behind me, standing far too close. Stay away, you idiots. I don't want to find that, thanks to you, I've just signed up for the great game of chance. Pick a card, any card. Test your luck.

It was resolved quickly enough. The old man's questions were answered, he moved on and the knot of people untangled. Two weeks ago, when the chance of catching the virus was probably higher than now, I would have thought little of it, but then I was less attuned to the dangers, I had less knowledge of how infectious this virus is – many times more so than flu – and I had read fewer accounts of people gasping for life in ICUs, waiting for a doctor to decide if they deserved a ventilator.

I decided to calm myself down by going for a gentle walk. As it was high time I properly acquainted myself with our new bubble, I went home, looked up Google Maps and traced a circle 300 metres in radius from our apartment block – the area where, according to the latest decree, we can go for exercise.

Our new world is a fraction of the size of our postal district of 00153 Roma, which is three and half kilometres across. We're now wholly severed from Testaccio across the river, let alone the city centre. As it happens, this side of the river has a long history of separation from the rest. In Rome's early days it was another country – Rome's territory was east of the Tiber while the west bank belonged to the city of Veii, whose faint ruins can still be seen in an area of parkland twenty kilometres to the north. On our side of the river people would have spoken Etruscan, a language which appears not to have been Indo-European, making it as distant from Latin as English is from Tibetan or Amharic Ethiopian. Until recently the Trasteverini had their own distinct dialect and considered themselves the only true Romans.

Studying the map of our new bubble, I saw things could be much worse. We're lucky to live right beneath the Gianicolo Hill. There are two stairways that we can still climb, both of them steep enough to get the blood moving. The first is in the small green area next to our apartment, which I've described in an earlier entry, and this was where I began today. As usual I brought my camera. Years ago, I bought a macro lens that I hardly ever found use for but now I'm glad to have it. When I try to capture spring flowers and tiny beetles, I find my own world seems a little less shrunken. These creatures aren't troubled by the coronavirus. The only effect it will have had on them is to make the air they absorb less polluted.

The second stairway extends upwards from the next street along from ours, the Viale Glorioso. It's very wide and though there are often one or two bored-looking Romans sitting there, risking the wrath of the authorities, there's plenty of room to step round them. One flight of steps has faint remnants of paint: orange and dark red that was daubed there nineteen years ago, in celebration of Roma football team's last victory in the Serie A.

Once again, the lockdown made me notice things that I normally walk past with hardly a glance. The slopes of the Gianicolo Hill have long been a green part of Rome. Julius Caesar had gardens here, where he's thought to have entertained Cleopatra, and in more recent times there were elegant villas and parks where wealthy Romans went to escape the din of the city. After Rome became the capital of a united Italy in 1870, and began expanding to fit its new role, roads were built here, winding their way up the slope, faced by grand houses. This was a better time than is often remembered. There was some corruption and destruction – a shameful number of ancient remains were lost in the building mania – but the economy thrived and the country had a free and lively democracy. It must have been an exciting time, as a new European country found its feet. Walking down the Via Dandolo and the Via Casini, I was struck by how the villas seemed to exude confidence. Many are beautiful, with wonderful details that look back to when Rome had last been the capital of all Italy, a millennium and a half earlier. Their inhabitants would have never imagined that their world would soon end, with the horror of the First World War and then the corruption and incompetence of that nationalist populist movement of a century ago: Fascism.

Touring our new bubble had worked, and I walked home in a much calmer state of mind than before. When I got back, we all agreed that from now on we'll plan our meals a week ahead, so I can avoid taking my chances at the supermarket more often than I have to. And I won't be going back to the place run by the family dynasty for a long time. The dismal one that has dreary brands and wide spaces between the food shelves will do just fine.

Writing on walls

This morning, when I went round the corner from our flat
for my daily walk, I noticed, on the side of a metal box that's
something to do with measuring traffic, a small poster.
It has probably been there for a while and it depicted a

green-coloured virus with a malevolent-looking face, while underneath was written, in English, 'Fuck Coronavirus'. It's a sentiment I couldn't agree with more.

I wasn't surprised to see it. Romans frequently vent their feelings on the walls of their city. They've done so since classical times and it's no accident that *graffiti* is an Italian word. During the Renaissance, several well-worn classical sculptures became known as the talking statues and formed a kind of Democracy Wall. On them, Romans would daub ferociously scornful tirades against the papal authorities, supposedly uttered by the statues. In one of these debates the statue Pasquino complained that he had been insulted in a most offensive way and another statue asked what the insult had been. Had he been called a liar or a thief? A cuckold or a forger? A fornicator who had got some poor woman pregnant? No, replied Pasquino, the insult was far, far worse. He had been called a cardinal.

Sometimes these statues, which are still in place, speak again, and I've seen them covered with diatribes directed at present-day politicians. But the feelings that Romans display on walls can also be very personal. Attached to the papal city wall not far from where we live is a small plaque that reads: *In September 2005 on this corner Alessandro and Anna met again, and a great love was born.*

A wall beside a bus stop near to us, which has an old relief of the Virgin Mary above a collection box marked 'Bread for the orphans', is covered with numerous inscriptions, all giving thanks for prayers heard.

And then there's the street art. Rome is rich in this and in some areas, such as Ostiense and San Lorenzo, people live surrounded by images. Some are poorly done, some are beautiful and many are uniquely Roman.

An apartment block in Testaccio has one wall decorated with an immense wolf.

I once passed an electrical box on which had been stencilled the picture of a playing card showing Pope John Paul II, beneath which was written, 'King of Popes'.

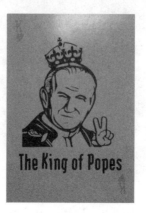

In Pope Francis' early, more popular days, I saw an image of him pulling open his robes to reveal a Superman costume beneath, with an *F* for Francis rather than an *S*.

Some of the artworks are very funny. I saw a whole series of pictures of the Virgin Mary and baby Jesus operating various types of equipment. In one, titled *Saint Madonna of Cinematography – lights, camera, action and so it will be*, Mary holds a cine camera and baby Jesus a light meter and a clapperboard.

A good deal of Rome's street art is critical of authority in a way that would have made Renaissance Romans proud, such as a stencil by one of Rome's most renowned street artists, Hogre. It is of Rubens' painting of Saint Peter receiving the keys to heaven, to which Hogre has added three young women and made it disturbingly sexual.

Or a poster, once again of the Madonna and baby Jesus, in which both have clothes pegs over their noses, and which is titled, *Saint Mary of the Clothes Peg – save us from the stink of cursed money.*

A stencilled image from some years back showed a monkey suspending a banana in front of his own eyes, and had the caption, *Vote Berlusconi.*

Another poster, produced by the Italian neo-fascist group, Zenit, was titled *Se Non Vai Dalla Democrazia, è La Democrazia che Viene da Te!* (If you're not for democracy, democracy will come for you!) and had a picture of a B-52 dropping dozens of bombs.

This last dates back to the 2003 Gulf War, an event that all Romans, whether their politics were extreme or moderate, right or left wing, were overwhelmingly against. Peace flags were hung from windowsills all across the city and it was the only time when, as someone with a northern-looking face, I felt a little self-conscious, though once I'd explained that I wasn't keen on the war either, suspicions towards me would soon vanish. Once we wheeled our baby son Alexander about the town clutching a tiny peace flag – he liked the colours – and he was applauded in the street.

Judging by all that has happened in the Middle East since 2003 – ISIS, brutal civil wars in Iraq and Syria – I'd say the Romans were quite right about the Gulf War. Now from windowsills, including several in our new bubble, there hang hand-drawn posters that declare, '*Andrà Tutto Bene*' (Everything will be fine). Let's hope the Romans are as right now as they were in 2003.

My family, tiny nation

This morning we had another scare. Alexander pushed a note under his closed door to say that he was self-isolating. He'd woken to find he had no sense of taste – one among various possible signs of the start of the coronavirus. I felt angry, not with him but that all our caution had been futile.

We set about separating ourselves from contact with him, familiar after our efforts when Shannon first returned from Canada. I filled a washbag with toothbrush, toothpaste and shaving things to keep them removed from our shared bathroom. How could Alexander have caught it, I wondered? There was the time he'd run into an old friend with his dog and they'd gone for a walk, but that had been a good while ago. He's gone shopping at the supermarket once or twice, but far less often than I have. It seemed very unlucky.

The answer, happily, was that he hadn't caught it after all. I first began to wonder when, through his closed door, he told us that it wasn't so much that he had no sense of taste but rather that he had an odd taste in his mouth. A few days ago he had developed a painful cyst behind his ear and yesterday we contacted our local Roman GP, who asked us to send him a photo and then, very efficiently, emailed us a long code number, which we took along with Alexander's health card to the chemist's at the end of the road, who in turn gave us antibiotics. A childhood memory came to me of having had a strange metallic taste in my mouth when on a course of antibiotics. As luck would have it, Shannon's sister-in-law in Toronto is a pharmacist. When we gave her the name of what Alexander has been taking, she at once confirmed my suspicions. This particular antibiotic is known for affecting sense of taste. We were virus-free after all.

There's nothing like a nasty scare disproved to make the world seem a brighter, warmer place. Touch wood – and I'm touching it now – things are beginning to look up. To everyone's great delight, our friend Yvonne in Amsterdam says she's feeling better. So are two old friends in London who have also come down with the virus. Barbie has recovered. The number of deaths here is still horrific, but the curve of new cases is coming down. If we stay careful and avoid going to the family dynasty supermarket with the bank of Easter eggs, we have a good chance of avoiding this nasty disease. An official in the Italian government announced only yesterday that, if people follow the rules, they could be relaxed in May.

I sense we're now entering a new phase. After the adrenalin, amazement and panic of the early lockdown, we'll now be in for a slower time of patient waiting. It's begun auspiciously. This morning we discovered that the French bakery, although still closed to customers coming in from the street, is now offering online delivery. Alexander is delighted. This lockdown will be a long, slow process but I'm confident we'll get through it. Our children have been calm and the ones who have been most worked up so far are Shannon and me. Both of us have occasional panics about the virus, while Shannon is also under great pressure from her online teaching. Matters are helped now that she has her work desk in the sitting room, where it's close to the Wi-Fi modem, but the recording is still very time-consuming, all the more so because she's meticulous about doing it well. Yesterday she found that three class lectures she'd spent a whole day recording hadn't been uploaded onto the website – probably because it's in such demand – and she had to do them all again.

For the most part we've all been getting on pretty well – but then we're used to being something of an island, thanks to who we are. Shannon is Canadian but has lived in Europe since she was in her twenties. I'm British but have lived in Rome for eighteen years. Now, thanks to my mother's past – fleeing from Germany in 1933 (her family was Jewish and her father was blacklisted for being a vehement critic of the Nazis) – I'm German, too. I was given my citizenship by the German ambassador here over coffee and cakes. She made a short speech about how it wasn't easy to be German, as the name was forever associated with another – Auschwitz – which I found very moving. We had been welcomed by the German government at the very moment when I felt my own government had turned its back on us.

As to our children, they could hardly be more complicated. They're Canadian citizens but not Canadians. They're British citizens but not British. They're German citizens but not Germans – though Alexander, inspired by his new passport, has learned some of the language. They were brought up here and they speak Italian, but they're not Italians either. Theresa May would dismiss us all as citizens of nowhere.

Yet I feel we're very lucky. We may have different passports but we like the same films and books, the same food, and we enjoy visiting the same places for the same reasons. I have a feeling that this strange time will not drive us apart but will bring us closer. In fact, I have a small confession to make. Coronavirus permitting, Alexander will leave home to start at university next autumn – a moment both Shannon and I have rather been dreading. Terrible though the reason for it is, I'm glad that we are having this time all together.

What brought us to Rome: a film that was never made

A few days ago, the UK government urged all British citizens to return home while they still could. I very much doubt they were thinking of us. We're all Italian residents and Shannon, of course, isn't even British. I have to say the thought had never occurred to me to go back. This is our home now.

If there's a single thing that brought us here, it was probably a film that was never made. My father, Nigel Kneale, was a screenwriter, originally from the Isle of Man, who became very involved with BBC television in its early days – he's best remembered for a series of science fiction dramas entitled *Quatermass* – and who later branched into scripts for feature films. In 1969, when I was eight years old, he was commissioned to write an adaption of a recent novel by James Clavell, *Tai-Pan*, which was about British traders in China during the First Opium War. It was decided, no doubt for reasons of cost, to shoot it not in East Asia but at the Cinecittà studios in Rome. My father was told by his agent that the film would probably never be made but at least it might get him to Italy, and the agent was right on both counts. The film's American producer and Italian producer, Martin Ransohoff and Carlo Ponti, didn't get along and my father was flown out several times to negotiate between the two. At first he came alone, then he managed to bring my mother, and finally, at the tail end of August, he smuggled us all down.

Looking back, I'm surprised by the impression Rome made on me. Late August isn't the best time to visit the city, as it's hot and sticky and most of the restaurants are closed, but I loved it. Ever since I can remember, I've been fascinated by history and I was entranced by this place, where you could see layer upon layer of the past piled on top of one another, like strata in rocks.

One of the sights that made the greatest impression on me was the church of San Clemente, not far from the Colosseum. Part of a monastery belonging to a group of Irish monks, it's a beautiful building that is little changed from when it was constructed in the twelfth century, but more remarkable is what its archaeology-minded Irish prior, Joseph Mullooly, discovered underneath. First, he found the aisles of a buried church, dating from the fourth century, with numerous wall paintings that contain the earliest known examples of written Italian. Lower again, where one can hear an underground stream rushing by, he found the rooms of a classical Roman townhouse, that had probably been used by early Christians for their meetings. He found a stretch of ancient Roman alleyway – so narrow that it still seems sinister – on the other side of which was a temple of Mithras, complete with dining benches and statuary.

And all of this was in a city of vivid colours, of friendly people, of rich scents – the smell of late-summer umbrella pines can still take me back to that moment – and the best food that I'd ever tasted. I have no memory of saying this (I was only eight), but according to my parents I told them then that I felt at home in Rome and it was where I wanted to live.

After that visit a part of me was always wondering how I might get back to Rome. I managed it a few times on trips around Europe and then, when I was in my mid-twenties, I lived here for a year. That was the moment when I was finally able to move beyond my tourist impressions and see what the city was really like. Rome was a very different city back in 1987. Its monuments hadn't been cleaned up and it had a dingy, smoke-stained appearance. There were frequent power cuts and telephone conversations from my apartment would abruptly come to a halt when the phone socket – a big round thing the size of a fist – fell out of the wall.

And there was the bureaucracy. Though I tried hard, I never did get my permit to stay. Withdrawing money from my account could take an hour and banks looked like cinemas, with rows of seats for customers to wait their numbered turn. Yet, despite all of this, I loved living in the city and would have stayed longer except for the work. The only option I could find was teaching English as a foreign language, which was repetitive and badly paid, and after a year I'd had enough. But Rome is a place that gets under your skin. More than a decade later, now married, I came back. Shannon and I had intended to have an adventure for a year or so but, eighteen years on, we're still here.

I wouldn't say Rome is for everyone. Anybody thinking of coming to live here should beware. The bureaucracy, though it's much better than it was in 1987, is still mysterious and time-consuming. You never quite know whether you'll strike efficiency or the opposite. Your car will become covered with scratches and dents. You'll find people can be kind and warm, or wholly selfish – sometimes, confusingly, the same people. You'll constantly have to watch out for cheating, mostly on a small and fairly harmless scale. You'll think the Romans are monstrous drivers – which they are. At times you'll feel driven a little insane by the noise and the chaos.

But it's the right place for us. Among all the changes this virus has brought – terrible, less terrible and relatively benign – is a very tiny one: it has made me realize as never before that this city is my home. All in all, there's nowhere else I'd rather be locked down.

In pizza we trust

This morning there was a piece about an Air Canada flight attendant who came down with the coronavirus, along with seven other air staff who'd been on the same flight. As well as feeling extremely sick, she also felt guilty. She had given the disease to her husband and two daughters and feared she'd unwittingly infected many passengers before she began to show symptoms. 'We're the super-spreaders, as people frantically fly home,' she said. The flight on which she was sure she'd caught the disease, and which had 450 passengers, was on the Toronto–Frankfurt route. I'm very glad Shannon came home early – if she'd delayed a few days she might have brought the virus home with her.

The lockdown is now in its fourth week and it's beginning to feel as if our lives have always been like this. Aside from occasional panics I'm beginning to find it, in some strange way, almost soothing. We don't have to worry about making plans – what to do this weekend, this Easter, this summer? – as no plans are possible. It's a little like an immensely long train journey – no use getting impatient or counting the days, as it will make no difference. You have to concentrate on the now. Is this how a lifer in a comfortable Scandinavian jail comes to feel? Are we becoming institutionalized?

Eventually, of course, all of this has to come to an end, and when it finally does, what I'd most like to do is to take a walk right around the city and then go for a pizza. If we have a favourite local pizzeria it is Da Ivo, and when we've been away for the summer we always go there to celebrate our return. It's a large, cavernous restaurant with a series of rooms extending deep under a Trastevere apartment block, along with a few tables on the street outside that are much sought after in hot weather. It is a classically Roman place – inexpensive, loud, friendly, hurried – and if you look closely, you'll see that the walls are painted yellow-orange and dark red: the colours of Roma football team.

Over the years we've grown to know the people at Da Ivo pretty well and they're a good lot. When Alexander was reaching an age when he first wanted to go out with friends, they'd go to Da Ivo. Not all restauranteurs would want a table of noisy, penny-counting fifteen-year-olds, but they were always made to feel welcome. One of the waiters once told us that he was going on a trip with his son to London and, in my bad written Italian, I emailed him advice on practicalities and things to see. Ever since then we've had extra privileges when it comes to getting a table and when we've finished our meal there's a curious ritual over the bill: the total is crossed out and we're given an enormous discount, which we answer by giving a vastly excessive tip.

We rarely get takeaway from there, as the pizza is never so good once it's sat cooling in a box, but on the occasions when we have done, and I've sat waiting for our pizzas to be ready, watching the pizza chef at work, I've felt honoured, as I swear this is one of the great sights of Rome – along with watching the colours change on the dome of Saint Peter's at dusk. It's done with a speed and simplicity that's the mark of a chef who knows his work perfectly. Da Ivo's pizzas are Roman-style, with thin crusts, and the lumps of dough that form the base are surprisingly small. The cook rolls them out flat, lines them up and quickly scatters ingredients over them that never look like enough, but when the pizza's ready they're ample. There's often one ingredient I don't expect – a little parmesan or an extra dash of oil. Then they're scooped up with the spatula on a long pole and into the wood oven they go. There'll be a dozen or so in there, all having been in for different lengths of time, but out they come, one by one, all perfect.

What would I have if we could go there tonight? I'd start with a bowl of pale cannellini beans, which look as dreary as can be but are delicious, and salad with rocket and cherry tomatoes. As for pizza, Da Ivo has two that I find particularly tasty: the Del Vecchio, which has tomato sauce, aubergine and bacon, and the eccentrically named Buffalo Bill, which has tomato sauce, cherry tomatoes and buffalo mozzarella. Choosing is always a dilemma, but in the end I usually go for the Buffalo Bill and I'm never disappointed. Oh, and I'll have a flask of your simple but delightful chilled house red, please.

Of course, Da Ivo is by no means the only pizzeria in Trastevere. Among various others is Ai Marmi (On the marble): a large and popular place on Viale Trastevere not far from the river. It has big marble tables (hence the name) and, in a fine example of Roman gallows humour, is generally called 'the slab' – as in morgue. It specializes in bean dishes for starters and it isn't bad, though I find the pizza a little lacklustre. Or there's Dar Poeta, on a quiet street in the medieval part of Trastevere. Here you can get a pretty good pizza, though it's become rather touristy over the years, and we once found our order taken by a waitress who was on a working holiday from Sweden.

Da Ivo's greatest rival, at least in my eyes, is across the river in Testaccio: the legendary Da Remo. This is even more Roman than Da Ivo, if such a thing were possible. Come after 7.30 p.m. and you'll join a long queue. Come after 8.30 and you'll be waiting outside for half the evening. Once you're finally let in, service is not unfriendly but proceeds at breakneck speed. Cutlery, paper napkins and bread clatter onto the table almost before you've sat down. It's not a spot to dither over your order. Da Remo is a deceptive place. The pizza menu is short and seems as dull as one could imagine, with all the classic toppings and nothing else. But then you taste the pizza... I don't want to be disloyal to Da Ivo, but Da Remo's pizzas are sublime – and for no reason that I can pinpoint. The crust, which is Roman-style thin, is perfect, and so is whatever goes on top. This is not a place that skimps on ingredients. But don't, I warn you, linger chatting once you've finished and the plates have been whisked away. Your occupation is strictly temporary and you'll soon be brought the bill and asked to pay it.

And then there's the very opposite of all of these places, Seu Illuminati, meaning Seu the enlightened. Seu himself, its manager, can usually be found there, sitting by the bar, and his face is everywhere, on the walls and on every menu. A little egotism is forgivable as he's created a remarkable place. Unlike Da Ivo or Da Remo, there are no pictures of Roma footballers or prints of old Rome scenes on the walls, and all is fashionably sparse, with neon lights spelling out 'In Pizza We Trust'. The pizzas match the decor. The menu changes each month and includes novel combinations, such as Gricia – a Roman pasta sauce with bacon, pepper and pecorino cheese – and coffee. The prices are higher than Da Ivo but they're far from extortionate and the place is so popular that you often have to reserve weeks ahead. But a little while ago, to our own surprise, we managed to book a table at the last moment. I was delighted, as we had something to celebrate: that day Alexander had received an offer from a university that he'd love to go to. And it was here, as we tucked into a quite delicious dessert pizza with coconut, almond and lime, served on a high platter, that Shannon rang us from Canada on WhatsApp and told us that, as of midnight, we'd be locked down. It seemed such a strange and ridiculous idea that the three of us burst out laughing.

I do hope all these pizzerias will reopen when we're finally released. I have no doubt that in Rome, as all across the world, there will be many places that won't make it. I've read business headlines prophesying that it will be a case of survival of the fittest, but I suspect it will be more a case of survival of the fattest: companies that happen to have cash in the bank right now, and haven't just taken out a big loan to upgrade or expand. For Rome's restaurants the timing of the virus couldn't be worse, as Easter, now just around the corner, is the busiest tourist season. For waiters and other staff, many of whom struggle to get by from one payday to the next, this will be a desperately anxious time. All in all, it's hard to imagine how the world will look when the lockdown ends, but I have no doubt it will be greatly changed.

The strange story of the Tomato King

A few days ago, Sara, who runs the fruit and vegetable stall with her father, Bruno, and her boyfriend, Matteo, texted me with exciting news: the market was to reopen again. This morning I went and found it transformed from its old self. The stalls were marked off with barriers of yellow tape to keep customers back, there was a designated entrance and exit, and socially distanced customers were formed into a long queue. This proved less daunting than it first seemed. Each stall was allowed one person at a time and, as Sara and Matteo had none, I was ushered straight through.

Though I'm very fond of our market, I wouldn't say it's the best in Rome. It's fairly small and can be overpriced. The one across the river in Testaccio is better. Both reflect their neighbourhoods. Trastevere, though it was once one of the poorest neighbourhoods in Rome, is fairly affluent these days, and has a good number of gullible foreign residents and tourists. By contrast, relatively few foreigners stray into Testaccio, which has little in the way of sights, and which – though it's becoming gradually more gentrified – is a tougher area.

It was tough two thousand years ago. In classical times Testaccio was a neighbourhood of dockworkers who laboured at the nearby river port (whose remains can still be seen beside the Tiber) or in one of the warehouse shopping emporiums nearby, of which the eroded walls of one still weave their way between modern apartment blocks. Testaccio's most remarkable monument, though, is the one that gives the area its name: Monte Testaccio (pottery hill). It's a place few tourists think of visiting today but it was a must for all self-respecting Victorian visitors, who wanted to be awed with a sense of Rome's immense longevity.

But I should explain. Most of the amphorae that came to classical Rome from the far reaches of its empire were recycled, but a minority, which contained oil from Spain and North Africa, could not be reused. Dockworkers poured their contents into barrels, broke them into two and then chucked them onto a heap of others. After this had been done for six centuries the heap had grown into a good-sized hill, which still towers over the buildings all around. These days it's flanked by car repair shops, nightclubs and restaurants, some of which have a glass display on their back walls, through which one can see row upon row of amphorae halves, neatly stacked.

When Rome's empire collapsed and the city declined, Testaccio disappeared, its buildings crumbled away and it became an unpopulated area of fields and vineyards. With the reunification of Italy and the city's revival after 1870, though, it sprang back to life. A huge slaughterhouse was built there, which now contains cafes and exhibitions, and it quickly took on much the same character it had fifteen centuries earlier. It's a strongly Roman area and on the rare occasions when Roma football team win the Serie A (which usually happens in a holy year – a clear case of divine match-fixing) there's nowhere that celebrates more noisily. And the Testaccians know their food. The area has many of the best traditional Roman restaurants in the city, including Da Felice, Da Bucatino, Perilli, the aforementioned legendary pizzeria Da Remo, and – if you like meat, as it's beside the old slaughterhouse and they serve little else – Checchino dal 1887.

And there's the market. We've been here long enough to see this go through great changes, which encapsulate all that's best and worst about Rome. When we first came here it was a basic place, housed in a vast, rambling shed – dark, dingy and none too clean. Yet the prices were very reasonable and the fruit and vegetables, the meat and fish and cheeses were as good as any in Rome. My favourite stall sold only tomatoes. The owner had a slightly mournful, world-weary look to him, and when I asked him how he was, he would always answer, a little gloomily, 'Da favola' (Fabulous). Rather unimaginatively, we referred to him as the Tomato Man. In Testaccio he was known as *il re del pomodoro*, or the Tomato King, and with good reason as he sold some four-dozen varieties. On one occasion I found myself waiting behind two smart-looking types who told him, self-importantly, that they were from one of Rome's smartest restaurants and then, with a sense of laying down a challenge, demanded to know what tomatoes would go with a particular kind of fish. The Tomato Man didn't reply but simply pointed.

The Tomato King

It was soon after the 2008 crash that I understood there was another side to the Tomato Man. Somehow, we had begun talking about bankers and I saw a gleam come into his eyes. 'What we need now,' he told me, 'is a Robespierre.' Soon after this the market was moved from its old site to a newly constructed building a few blocks away. When I went there for the first time, I found it a revelation. Larger than its predecessor, it was beautifully designed, with subtly shaded glass panels in the roof that filled it with light. All was spotlessly clean. The stalls had cooling systems to keep produce fresh. There was a central courtyard with a cafe and tables, and one could look down into an excavated area, containing classical era remnants unearthed when the new market was built. There was even a spacious underground car park for customers. I no longer had to drive round the neighbourhood hoping to find an empty spot (Testaccio is notoriously bad for parking) and then heave bags of shopping half a mile to where I'd found one.

As to food, there were more fruit and vegetable stalls than ever, along with butchers, fishmongers, delicatessens, bakeries, fresh pasta makers and a good number of places offering wonderful street food. But one thing was missing. Though I scoured every corner of the place there was no sign of the Tomato Man.

Eventually I found out what had happened. Having dallied with the idea of moving to the new market, he'd eventually decided against it and, despite an order to leave, as the old market was to be emptied for demolition, he'd declared that he would not be moved and he'd set up his stall surrounded by tomatoes. The authorities overreacted. Perhaps he had an old enemy somewhere. They sent police cars, sirens blaring, forcibly removed him and then gave him a large fine.

I saw him a few times, walking around the new market, looking rather nattily dressed, talking to stallholders. I once told him that the market wasn't itself without him. He gave me a sad look and told me, 'My son was so angry that he's never eaten a single tomato since. Not one.'

That was several years ago, but lately the Tomato Man has again been in my thoughts. A few months back, before the coronavirus came into the world, I drove to Testaccio market to do some shopping. Over time I'd noticed that the places for customers in the car park had grown steadily fewer, as more spots were rented out to private car owners. Now all of a sudden there were no places at all. It was no mystery why – I saw a whole section had now been assigned to a car rental firm. The attendant, who looked hassled, did his best and said I could use one of the private spaces so long as I stayed no more than an hour. When I went up into the market and told one of the stallholders what had happened, he said he couldn't bear to think of it as it made him so angry. When I asked him how such a thing could have occurred – that the car park specifically created for the market could be sold off space by space, until there was hardly one left – he told me, *'Benevenuto a Rome'* (Welcome to Rome). For a moment I felt as if I could hear a voice drifting across the years, 'What we need now is a Robespierre.'

Our local Syrian temple

Our bubble may be rich in bugs and turn-of-the-century villas, but there's not much from classical Rome to be seen here. Julius Caesar's gardens are long gone, and on my daily walks there's only one ancient site that I pass by. This is on Via Dandolo, beside our nearest park, Villa Sciarra, and is close enough to our home that we can almost see it from our balcony. Whenever I've gone by the gates have been locked and I have yet to see anyone inside. One could probably gain access by applying to the *soprintendenza dei beni culturali* (the body that looks after cultural sites) but I've never been tempted to try. The sign on the gate states that it's a Syrian temple and, peering through, I can see that there's not a great deal left – just brick walls, mostly low, of a long, narrow structure, much overgrown. The rearmost part, which is built against the slope of the Gianicolo Hill, is the best preserved, and has several niches where statues of gods would once have stood. One part is in danger of collapse and has been propped up with supports.

Our local Syrian temple.

Though I haven't been very curious about this little temple before now, this morning, with my eyes refocussed by the lockdown, I decided to find out what I could, and here is the essence of what I've discovered. In the very earliest days of Rome there was, just beside this spot, a grove of trees and a small spring that were a place of worship to a minor goddess of woods and water, named Furrina. In the first century AD a new temple was built here, now to Syrian gods, though a link with the nymph Furrina was kept. In the second century this temple was lavishly reworked with the help of a rich Syrian immigrant named M. Antonius Gaionas. Two hundred years later the temple was destroyed by fire, only to be hastily rebuilt soon afterwards, if in a plainer way. A short time after this it was attacked by Christians, its statues were smashed and it was abandoned for good, long to be forgotten. The only reason it is known now is that, fifteen centuries later in 1906, a lodge was built for the intendant of the new Villa Sciarra park, and the temple's remains were discovered.

As that all seems a little dull, I will now try and put a little flesh on these historical bones. The nymph Furrina goes back to the very earliest era of Rome's history, and for that matter she harks back to some of humanity's earliest beliefs, of spirits that inhabit haunting or useful places. By the first century AD she was largely forgotten. By then people were fast losing interest in Rome's first gods, which were watched over by priesthoods of stuffy, prestige-seeking aristocrats, and offered no emotional exuberance nor any hope of an afterlife in paradise. The old gods hadn't kept up with Rome, which had grown from a small Italian town of timber and bricks to a marble city of more than a million inhabitants. Many of these inhabitants were immigrants, both slaves and free, who came from every corner of the Roman Empire, and no district was more cosmopolitan than Trans Tiberim (meaning 'across the Tiber' – now Trastevere).

Trans Tiberim's temples were as diverse as its people, and on the hillside just above it, one immigrant group of Roman Syrians, who were probably connected with the port of Berytus (Beirut), built a temple. It was dedicated to several of their gods, but was probably associated most strongly with Osiris who, like another new religious figure of this time – Jesus Christ – promised his followers an afterlife in heaven. The Syrians weren't satisfied with their temple and after a number of decades they rebuilt it, lavishly, with the help of M. Antonius Gaionas. As luck would have it, we know a little about this man. This was clearly his intention, as he left a number of inscriptions recording his achievements. One of these was found at Rome's seaport, Portus, suggesting he was probably a merchant and ship owner – a risky business, but highly profitable if you were shrewd and lucky.

What was life like for a driven, successful immigrant businessman trying to make it in the empire's capital? Some ideas can be found by reading the third satire by one of Imperial Rome's greatest and most poisonous poets, Juvenal. Born in a small town near Montecassino, Juvenal considered himself thoroughly Roman, and deeply resented the immigrants from the east whom he believed were flooding his homeland and depriving him of a livelihood. His third satire is a raging and profoundly racist diatribe which, if one substitutes *migrant* for *Greek* (by which Juvenal meant any easterners, including Syrians), would satisfy the most alt-right nationalist populist of our time. Here are a couple of quotes to give a taste...

> Now let me turn to that race which goes down so sweetly with our millionaires, but remains my special pet aversion, and not to mince my words. I cannot, citizens, stomach a Greek Rome...

Juvenal's easterners are cheats, flatterers, whores, and seducers of good Roman women. Most of all, they take every job in town.

> Quick wit, unlimited nerve, a gift of the gab that out-smarts a professional public speaker – that's them. So what do you take that fellow to be? He's brought every profession with him – schoolmaster, rhetorician, surveyor, artist, masseur, diviner, tightrope-walker, magician or quack, your hungry Greekling is all by turns. Tell him to fly – he's airborne!*

Gaionas did his best to impress the crusty, disdainful world he was trying to break into. On no fewer than three inscriptions he proclaims that he held a lowly position in Rome's fire and police watch, which was little to boast about and indicates how eager he was to be seen as a good Roman citizen. His epitaph records that he was also an official in the Imperial Cult (a patriotic organization for worshipping

---

* Juvenal, *The Sixteen Satires*, trans. Peter Green (1967).

the emperor as a god). Gaionas would have been very familiar with that age-old immigrant balancing act of trying not to seem too foreign to your new countrymen, yet not losing the friendship of your own community. So, he worked to impress his people by backing a splendid restoration of their temple. And, to show respect to the Romans, even though the temple was to a very foreign eastern set of gods, polite reference was made to the long-defunct cult of Furrina that had occupied almost the same spot.

Gaionas' splendid temple, though, proved less enduring than he would have hoped. Precise dates are hard to establish, but it was burned to the ground, almost certainly by Christians, of whom there were many in Trans Tiberim. This may have occurred in AD 356, when the imperial government closed all pagan temples, giving Christian zealots a chance to settle scores. The Syrian temple site was abandoned and the pool beside it filled in, but not for long. Soon afterwards the temple sprang back to life and it was wholly rebuilt, if in a plainer form than before. The early 360s saw a fascinating moment in Rome's history. A new emperor, Julian, seized power, and though his parents had both been Christian and he had been brought up as one, he loathed the religion and returned the empire to paganism. Accounts of this era, which is still seen through Christian-tinted spectacles, often portray the old pagan religions as so enfeebled that they succumbed to the return of Christianity a couple of years later with hardly a murmur, yet the Syrian temple on the Gianicolo tells a different story. Its congregation seized their opportunity under Julian and constructed what appears to be the very last pagan temple built in Rome. Their efforts were in vain. Barely eighteen months after he had taken power, Emperor Julian was dead, killed campaigning at Samarra in present day Iraq. Christianity regained ascendancy and Roman Christians stormed the new Syrian temple, smashing the statues of its gods. This time it would not recover.

Now Rome has a new group of immigrants from Syria, fleeing the brutal civil war there. Some of them have helped cheer up our lockdown. Shaza Sakar, who came to Rome from Syria when she was three, and went on to study at the university where Shannon teaches – John Cabot – set up a company called Hummustown, which prepares Syrian food to deliver for events and individuals. Shaza makes a point of employing recently arrived refugees from her country, to help them find their feet, which she has done for more than thirty people now. A few nights ago we ordered a delicious Hummustown meal of aubergine and beet dips, falafel, lamb sausages, salad with croutons, Arabic bread and, of course, hummus. It brought some welcome exoticism to these very Roman days.

I'm sure Gaionas would have been proud to think that, nineteen centuries in the future, one of his compatriots would be making her mark in Rome and helping her community here, just as he did. Tomorrow, when I go for my bubble walk, I'll look at the ruined walls of the Syrian temple with new curiosity. And when I next pass through the little green area by our apartment block, I'll wonder what else may lie buried beneath all those spring flowers, and what stories it may have to tell.

Tuesday the 7th of April

An atheist and the Catholic Church

I can't believe it's almost Easter. In three days it will be
Good Friday. With the lockdown there's little to show the
passing of time aside from the buds growing on the trees
outside the windows. Our children have been joking that
they can't wait for their spring break – when of course
everything will be just the same as it is now.

Normally, around this time a notice appears on the door
to our stairway, announcing an imminent visit by clerics
to bless our home. I usually completely forget and when I
hear a ring at the door I assume it's a delivery from the wine
shop, Bernabei, or another pair of scammers trying to copy
our gas bill, only to open the door and find myself looking
out at a smiling priest or a pair of nuns (it varies from year
to year). My children, if they're at home, hide in their rooms
while I, who doesn't have a religious bone in my body, feel a
strange need to feign piety, if only for the sake of politeness.

Rome still attracts plenty of pilgrims – one can see
numerous groups of them, often wearing something yellow,
which is the Vatican colour – but it certainly wasn't religion that drew us here. I'm the son of two atheists, one

descended from Manx Methodists and the other from German Jews, while Shannon, who was brought up in the tolerant Protestantism of Canada's United Church, is agnostic going on atheistic. When we first came to live here I assumed we'd have no dealings with the Catholic Church, but it hasn't proved quite so simple.

Our first encounter was through education. Both our children went to an Italian day care and though our oldest, Alexander, was keen to go straight into an English language school, our daughter, Tatiana, decided to follow her friends and went to a Catholic school that adjoined the day care. At the first parents' meeting, the priest headmaster assured us that teaching would involve no attempts at religious conversion. I realized that this wasn't strictly true one day when we were driving and I happened to play 'Let it Be' by The Beatles on the car stereo. When Paul McCartney sang about 'Mother Mary' I saw a strange look come into Tatiana's eyes and I knew the song meant altogether more to her than it did to the rest of us. Not that the school's teaching had its desired effect. Tatiana's older brother, who'd had no contact with Catholicism beyond attending the occasional Holy Communion ceremonies of his friends, was rather drawn to the religion for a time, but when Tatiana left her Catholic school after a year, she emerged a determined nonbeliever.

These days, of course, the Catholic Church is inextricably linked in many minds with paedophilia and sexual abuse. But then the papacy has often had an image problem, which hasn't been helped by the fact that across the centuries there have been so many pontiffs who were far from pious. There have been warrior popes, hungry for territory and power, who led papal armies in battle. There have been excessively family-minded popes, concerned to enrich their cousins and nephews – and sometimes their own children – and to found new dynasties. There have been pleasure-seeking popes who spent lavishly on good food and entertainments. There have been scheming popes, inflicting slow revenge on enemies. There have been lustful popes who took lovers, female and male, into their beds. There have been vanity popes, intent on leaving their mark with great monuments (and I have to say, Rome is all the better for them). After the rise of Protestantism sent the Church onto a narrower path, there were vehemently anti-Semitic popes, who deported Rome's Jews into a walled ghetto and drove them from all but the poorest professions in an attempt – unsuccessful – to force their conversion. In the 1930s and 40s there was a pro-Nazi pope, Pius XII.

We've been in Rome long enough to see the Church's ups and downs at first hand. I watched, but didn't join, the huge queues as around a million people waited for hours to file past the body of Pope John Paul II. We sensed Romans' increasing disdain for his successor, Benedict XVI, both for his conservative religious views and his failure to deal with the paedophile scandal. We watched the excitement that arose in the early days of Pope Francis, when he'd drive around the city in his modest Ford Focus and seemed a hip, radical pope like no other. Even then I doubted the Church's popularity would last very long. How could an institution whose core beliefs go back to the thirteenth century, if not earlier, connect with people today? Still, I was surprised by how quickly Francis' popularity waned.

Overall, though, Romans are proud that the papacy is a part of their city. I once found myself in a city cab on a fine day and made a remark about Rome's good climate. 'Of course it's good,' the cab driver replied briskly. 'We have the pope. You only have the queen.' It was a joke, but not entirely. I've heard Romans say that they don't have to worry about what sins they get up to because they're near to the pope – his geographical proximity is a guarantee of a place in paradise. Again, this is not entirely meant as a joke.

Romans' sense of ownership over the Church allows them to behave quite shamelessly. One Christmas Day some years back, I saw that a church that was always shut had finally opened its doors and I went in to have a look. Mass was being celebrated and, as the priest prayed, I heard a loud beeping when a member of the congregation's mobile phone started ringing. Rather than fumbling to switch it off, or fleeing in shame, the owner peered down to see who the call was from and then – as the priest did his best to keep talking – strode unhurriedly from the church, chatting loudly as he went. Nobody in the congregation seemed at all surprised.

Despite being the capital of Catholicism, Rome doesn't come across as a devout city. If anything, I'd say the city's role has diminished Romans' sense of piety. Centuries of fleecing pilgrims, rich and poor, has left Romans cynical. And by no means are all Romans believers. On several occasions I have been surprised to discover that someone who I assumed was religious isn't at all. One such Roman non-believer told me, 'Why make a noise about it? You never know, you might want to do business with the Church one day.' There's certainly plenty of business to be done. As well as some 900 churches, Rome contains numerous seminaries and other institutions that all need to be maintained, and their inhabitants fed and looked after.

Among all the representatives of Catholicism in the city, the most visible are nuns, who have much more of a public presence than priests. At the hospital up the hill from us, blood tests are taken by a German nun and though I was a little taken aback when I first saw her in her robes, wielding a syringe, I soon grew used to it. She was very kindly, but many Roman nuns can be tough. Shannon, when visibly pregnant with Tatiana, found herself in the post office at the end of a long queue and her appearance quickly sparked a debate among the others waiting. All were agreed that she should go straight to the front of the queue, with one exception: a hard-faced nun who insisted Shannon must wait her turn (she was outvoted). And if you're driving in Rome, keep a sharp eye out for small cars crammed with sisters, as they can be among the most aggressive drivers on the road.

In the main, though, I have to say that living in Italy has made me think better of Catholicism rather than otherwise. The Church may be intensely clannish, it may have a lust for ideological control, and it has turned a blind eye to appalling betrayals of trust by those within its ranks, and yet it does look after people, too. Before we came to Rome, we lived for a short time in a small town to the south-east of here, Alatri, in a house that we shared with an elderly woman named Marcella. Orphaned as a child – when she'd had a good few glasses of wine she once told us that her father had murdered her mother out of jealousy – she lived as a kind of unordained nun. The high point of her week was on Sunday when she helped out at the local church, and afterwards she'd come home and excitedly grab our hands to show how cold it had been there – and her hands would be freezing. The church gave her a role and made sure she wasn't forgotten.

In our neighbourhood medieval church, Santa Maria in Trastevere, at lunchtime each Christmas Day the nave is emptied of pews and is transformed into a restaurant, where the local poor and homeless are waited on by clergymen. There's an element of publicity about the event, which often appears in the news, but that doesn't alter the fact that it takes place. In the last few years, as part of his school curriculum, Alexander did some community work, teaching maths and Italian to refugee children, for the Trastevere organization set up to help the homeless, Sant'Egidio. When it was first set up in the late 1960s, it sought to give refugee children living unsettled lives a quiet place to do their homework, and this role was gradually extended to offering tutoring as well. For people who have nothing, and for whom education offers the only hope of advancement, I have no doubt this help can make a huge difference.

Sant'Egidio, and the Vatican too, are much involved in looking after Rome's homeless. And the Church's messages will give comfort to elderly Romans who feel afraid at this time. The atheist and cynic in me recalls that religions always do well during a time of plague – but if there's a little opportunism, there's also real generosity of spirit. Ultimately, I would say that the Catholic Church, like any vast institution, is as good and bad as the people who have been drawn into its ranks.

Friday the 10th of April

Breaking out and seeing Fascism

Last night we had another Zoom meeting with our friends and we were all badly in need of seeing different faces and hearing everybody's news. One of our friends was so cabin-fevered that he proposed that we should all get together for a secret drink in somebody's house. Nobody else was at all keen. The rules we're living by are in place for a good reason, and though we all assume we're clear of the virus, who's to know if one of us might have picked it up in some shop or supermarket, and would then spread it to the others, who would then spread it further? The penalties for infractions are tough now. A few days ago, a man from Testaccio was stopped in his car near the Circo Massimo – barely a kilometre from his home – and fined €3,000.

Still, I have to admit that, after a month locked down and two and a half weeks bubbled down, the thought of a change of view is tempting. Looking for insects in our green area, admiring the villas on the Via Dandolo, peering through the gates of the Syrian temple – it feels a very small world. Perhaps it's time to throw caution to the winds and burst out? Are you up for it? It's another beautiful day, with tree blossom just beginning to show itself, white and pink. Don't be alarmed. Try as they may, nobody can fine you on these pages. I know it's Good Friday, which is the busiest, maddest time in all the year to see Rome, but to hell with it. Let's walk and walk, for four thousand words, five thousand, six thousand, till our feet ache and we can hardly take another step. Let's see the whole city. Not postcard Rome. I'll show you some places that few visitors think of going to. What's that? With the lockdown everything will be closed? Don't worry, I give you my guarantee that it will all be open. The Italian government has decreed that we must stay within our bubbles. I now decree that, just for you, today will be a normal Good Friday.

Good Friday is a working day in Italy, of course, and a busy one. Let's give a wave to Roberto and Anna, struggling to serve the crowd of customers waiting to buy traditional Easter salami (with big chunks of fat). And as we pass the market let's give a 'Buongiorno' to Matteo, Sara and her father, Bruno, hurrying to sell potatoes, artichokes and other vegetables to go with everybody's Easter meal of lamb. Tomorrow will be busier still. On we go, across the frontier of our bubble. Even before the lockdown, this short street, Via di San Cosimato, was a frontier. Behind us is Piazza San Cosimato, with its bars and restaurants, our market and a children's playground – where I spent many an hour standing beneath the climbing frame in case Alexander or Tatiana fell off – which is the locals' Trastevere. Ahead,

Piazza di Santa Maria is tourist Trastevere, where visitors are happy to pay extra for a coffee where they can sit and look at the view. Then again, it is quite a view. Santa Maria in Trastevere is one of the most beautiful churches in Rome. But here's something few people know. It was built from spite. In the early twelfth century the church here was associated with the antipope, Anacletus II, and when he died and his rival and enemy, Pope Innocent II, gained control of Rome, Innocent had Anacletus' church demolished and wholly rebuilt. A prettier consequence of vindictiveness I've yet to see, and it's never looked better than now. The paintings on the facade, which had become very faded, were restored recently and you can now make out long-vanished details.

Our next stop is one of nostalgia. Let's make our way across the piazza, past the street buskers and the man launching huge detergent bubbles into the air, past the Ci-Lin Chinese restaurant, and down the quiet lane of Vicolo del Piede. See the door over there? It doesn't look like much now but it was once the entrance to a great Trastevere institution: the Pasquino English-language cinema. It's not easy to see films in their original language in Italy, as a law that dates back to the Mussolini era requires everything to be dubbed. The Pasquino was the city's only full-time English-language cinema, and it was unusual in another way, too. I was once in the audience here on a hot summer's night in the late 1980s when, as the film was rather dull, I happened to glance upwards and, to my surprise, I saw stars shining down. When the film ended, I looked up again and all I saw was ceiling, making me wonder if I'd imagined the whole thing. I had to go several more times before I looked up at the right moment and saw the roof silently swinging open. Sadly, the Pasquino is no more.

Here's more nostalgia. It's quite a maze round here, I know, and if you've ever wondered what classical Rome was like, look no further; these winding streets, faced by apartment blocks three or four or five floors high, are much as residential streets would have been in the ancient city – albeit cleaner. And here we are: Vicolo della Frusta. It was once a street of carriage-makers – hence the name, which translates, rather suggestively, as Whip Lane. Do you see the low building on the left, with a metal door opening onto the street? This was where Shannon and I first lived in Rome. It's not large inside, just one bedroom, and Alexander, who was here from babyhood to toddler-hood, had to sleep in a walk-in wardrobe, but we liked it. We lasted until the day came when we fixed a pink rosette to the front door: the Italian way of announcing the birth of a baby daughter. After that we definitely didn't fit.

Next I'd like to show you a scene of Roman glory. In truth there isn't as much of this as you might expect in Rome's long history. In the early days, as Rome rose from an obscure Italian town to a Mediterranean superpower, there was determination, a will to dominate and a good deal of cruelty, yet personally there's not much that I find likeable about the Romans' heroics. Up here, though, they did something that I truly can admire. It's a bit of a climb, I know, steps and then more steps, so let's pause for a moment by this grand fountain. If it looks familiar it's probably because you saw it in the opening scene of the film *La Grande Bellezza*, when a Japanese tourist suddenly dies of a heart attack. It's a vast fountain, with an immense out-pouring of water, because this is actually an entire river; it's the arrival point in the city of one of classical Rome's aqueducts, the Acqua Paola. In Rome's efficient, classical days the city had no fewer than eleven functioning aqueducts, of which three still work. They each have a grand arrival place – the other two are the Fountain of Moses, by Via Venti Settembre, and the Trevi Fountain. It's quite a view from up here and you can see the whole of Rome. Over to the right are the Alban Hills – Rome's local dormant volcanoes – and straight ahead are the Apennines. Those distant peaks covered in snow, where Romans go skiing, are just an hour's drive from here.

I'm tempted to make a short detour. A little south of here is a small, beautiful park, the Villa Sciarra, that nestles inside a corner of the old papal walls. You can see part of it from our flat. Walk through it early in the morning and you may come across one of Rome's more curious sights. First, you'll hear beautiful violin music emanating from behind trees up by the wall. As you come closer and the music grows louder you'll see a dog crouched on the slope beneath the walls, looking up with an air of great expectation. After a moment the music stops and a ball flies out of the greenery, bounces away and the dog dashes off in pursuit. The violinist, who's very talented, comes here with the twin purpose of practising away from his neighbours and walking his dog.

But we have no time for detours. Out through the papal wall we go, and down this short, noisy stretch of Via di San Pancrazio. And here it is – the scene of glory. It doesn't look much now, I know: a small, gravelly car park that opens up before us, V-shaped, and then extends ever wider into the greenery of another park beyond, which is one of Rome's largest, the Villa Pamphili, that stretches on for several miles. It feels so peaceful here, walking up the gentle slope between avenues of trees, towards a triumphal arch, and you'd never think this was once a scene of slaughter. If there's one single place where Italy was born as a united, independent country, free of foreign rulers, it's right here.

On an early June day in 1849, scores of Romans and other Italians died on this spot. It was a time of revolution. The pope, Pius IX, had fled into exile and France's new ruler, Louis Napoleon, had sent a powerful army to crush Rome's pro-unification government and put Pius back on his throne. During the night the French, using trickery, had seized a strategically key point. It was a country villa on high ground, of which nothing remains, where the triumphal arch now stands. The Roman commander, Giuseppe Garibaldi, knew that unless the villa was recaptured the city would be impossible to defend. Wave after wave of Italians came through a small gate at the beginning of what is now the car park and then ran up the slope, across open country where there was no cover to protect them from blistering French fire from the villa. Several times the Italians captured the villa only to lose it again, as it was impossible to defend from the other side. By evening the struggle was over and, after a few weeks of valiant defence, Rome fell and – the much hated – Pope Pius returned to power.

Yet, if the battle was lost, the slaughter in this pretty wooded area brought about success in the end. Until this time, Italian patriots had been viewed from abroad as divided and lacking commitment. The terrible battle that was fought here helped persuade influential foreigners, including British prime-minister-to-be William Gladstone, of the passion and justice of the Italian cause. To see how matters concluded, we need only retrace our steps and then turn left, passing busts of numerous heroes of Italian unification, till we reach the Piazza Giuseppe Garibaldi. The view here is even better than it was by the fountain. We're lucky it's still early in the morning, as on this spot you can get quite a shock. Every day at noon, soldiers of the Italian army wheel out an artillery piece from just below and fire off a blank round to signal the hour. It's extremely loud and, if you're not expecting it, it can really make you jump. And there's Garibaldi, looking splendid on his great horse. But here's another curiosity. Do you see how he's not facing ahead towards the city but disdainfully to the left, towards the Vatican? It's as if he's staring down the popes and telling them, 'Look who won.'

Giuseppe Garibaldi glowering in the direction of the Vatican.

This was certainly how the papacy saw matters. When, after six decades of icy non-relations between the popes and the Italian state, Mussolini negotiated a pact with the Church, one of the Vatican's first demands was that the statue of Garibaldi should be removed. It's not often that I agree with Mussolini, but on this occasion I do. Unwilling to show himself to be in the Church's thrall, he not only kept Garibaldi where he was, but he put up a new statue just down the road of Garibaldi's Brazilian wife, Anita, who was hardly less of a warrior than her husband. There she is, in a suitably heroic pose, on a rearing horse, a pistol in one hand and a baby in the other.

I think that's enough glory. Our next stop is the site of altogether more self-interested events – but then part of the charm of Rome's immense history is that it's so filled with instances of human weakness. Along the ridge of the Gianicolo Hill we go, down the steps and past the remains of Tasso's Oak, beneath which the sixteenth-century poet Torquato Tasso, who suffered greatly from depression, would sit in his last, troubled days. Long propped up and kept alive, the tree is now nothing more than a hollow, dead trunk and a few blackened, dead branches.

On down the hill to the river and there it is: an immense, circular chunk of stonework with battlements on the top. The Castel Sant'Angelo, originally the tomb of the Roman Emperor Hadrian, was so high and strongly built that it became Rome's citadel – the city's Bastille or Tower of London. You see that wall-like structure leading out from it to the left? That is a fine example of papal foresight. It's the *Passetto di Borgo* – a raised passageway, that leads all the way to Saint Peter's Basilica, almost a kilometre from here. It proved very useful on the morning of 6 May

1527, when Charles V's half-starved army rushed into the Vatican like a great scythe, killing everything in its path. As Pope Clement VII, who had been praying in St Peter's for longer than was wise, hurried along this escape route, he was spotted by Spanish troops, who took shots at him from below.

At this same moment there was an immense crush of desperate Romans fleeing in through the gate to the Castello – just over there. Pope Clement was consulted and, on being told that many of these citizens were of no military use, he had them thrown out, including women and children. What became of them is hard to know. But there was always room for those of the right kind. Cardinal Pucci was hauled up by a rope through a window and Cardinal Armellino was pulled over the battlements in a basket. As Romans across the city were murdered, raped, castrated, tortured and ransomed, life in the Castel Sant'Angelo wasn't too bad. There had just been time to bring in provisions before the enemy arrived, and the besieged had forty bullocks for meat, plenty of grain and rice, ham and cheese and some excellent Greek wine. But before we snigger and judge, perhaps we should ask ourselves, what would we have done? Would we have cast self-interest aside and walked out to share our fate with our fellow Romans? Or would we have stayed safe, guiltily sipping Greek wine?

Our apartment block, seen from the papal wall.

Our *portiera*, Cinzia: source of recipes and sanity.

Fascist-era lift in our apartment block.

Green area and papal wall
by our apartment.

Closely observed flowers,
bees and beetles.

Elegant early twentieth-century houses in our lockdown bubble.

Our local piazza, Santa Maria in Trastevere.

Roberto and Anna of our legendary local delicatessen, Antica Caciara.

Matteo, Sara and Bruno of Trastevere market, who brought fruit and veg to our door.

Deserted lockdown Rome.
Above: The Vittoriano. *Below*: Piazza Navona.

Empty Rome at dusk.
Above: Trevi fountain. *Below*: Spanish Steps.

Above: Piazza del Campidoglio with the Palazzo Senatorio – Rome's town hall – floodlit with the tricolore, Italy's flag, to raise people's spirits.

Left: Unlocked at last: Shannon and Alexander in the Piazza Navona on the day of our release.

Castel Sant'Angelo

You'd like to go to the Vatican? It's Good Friday, remember? D'you see the queue to go through security to Saint Peter's, that winds halfway round the square? As for the Vatican Museum, it's a long time since I've encouraged any visitor to go there, except during the very lowest of the low season. These days it's like a scrum, where you can hardly see the museum's wonders for the crowds brandishing selfie sticks and tour guides' batons. Some blame Dan Brown but I'd point the finger at Ryanair, EasyJet and Airbnb. The Vatican should really put a cap on numbers, for both the sake of its visitors and to protect its treasures – I can't believe all that damp breath is good for the frescoes in the Sistine Chapel and the Raphael rooms – but I see no sign of that happening. They're loathe to lose a euro of ticket income.

If it's all right with you, I'd rather go somewhere else, where I can guarantee there'll be hardly a tourist in sight, and which, in its way, is no less interesting. It also says a great deal about the darker side of Rome's recent history. First, we need to cross over the Ponte Cavour and walk alongside the river. But it's hard not to get sidetracked in Rome. Let's stop here, just for a moment and look through this window. This building, which was designed by the US architect Richard Meier – and has many detractors for its un-Roman, white exterior – houses one of the finest examples of Roman art: Emperor Augustus' Temple to Peace, the Ara Pacis. As well as mythological scenes, it depicts the imperial family processing to take part in a sacrifice. For anyone who's read Robert Graves' *I Claudius*, half the cast of characters is here: a big Italian family dynasty that had hit the jackpot as rulers of the empire, captured in stone before they turned murderously on one another.

Along with the statue of Anita Garibaldi, this is a rare instance where I'm willing to give a little praise to Mussolini (his draining of the Pontine Marshes, which helped overcome Italy's malaria problems is a third). The Ara Pacis had long before been broken into fragments, some of which were found during nearby excavations. Other sections had made their way into foreign museums and Mussolini made it a diplomatic priority to get them back. He wasn't always successful, and some segments of the temple we see today are copies of the originals, but it's wonderful to see the building standing.

Yet the restoration of the Ara Pacis came at a cost. The parts of the temple that were found here were discovered during the destruction of this neighbourhood of the city, which was demolished to excavate Emperor Augustus' tomb – whose rather disappointing remnants are just over there – and to make space for the hideous Fascist buildings all around us. This was one of many Roman neighbourhoods whose old houses, churches and piazzas were torn down, displacing over 100,000 Romans. Mussolini wanted to make Rome into a new Paris or Berlin, with wide, military-parade-sized boulevards, though Rome's charm was that it was the very opposite: a city of narrow streets and intimate spaces. We just crossed a prime example of Mussolini's vandalism: the Via della Conciliazione that leads to Saint Peter's. To build it, Mussolini destroyed a medieval area of long, narrow, winding streets. He also destroyed the drama of walking through these and suddenly emerging to find oneself in Saint Peter's Square, with Saint Peter's Basilica rising up behind.

So much for what Mussolini destroyed, what did he build? That's what we're going to see. We have to pass through Piazza del Popolo, which is where, for centuries, most pilgrims first entered the city. Do you see those two churches behind us, that look identical? They're actually an ingenious optical illusion, and one is larger than the other.

Out through the city walls we go, and here's our tram, number 2, as it's too far to walk. A short ride, a walk across the Ponte Duca d'Aosta, and here we are.

This is the Foro Olimpico, originally known as the Foro Mussolini, a broad expanse of Fascist display that, rather surprisingly, has survived intact. See the paving with *M* for Mussolini, and *Duce a Noi*. Over here, around the Marble Stadium, these statues were each made in a different Italian city. Though I have to say that rather than looking resolute and Fascist, many of the athletes look anxious and, dare I say it, rather camp.

Here, perfectly preserved, is a line of plaques that proclaim Fascism's supposed achievements, from the seizure of power to the conquest of Abyssinia. Rather than pull them down, the post-Fascist authorities simply added more, recording Fascism's fall and the rise of the Republic of Italy. And here, by the river, is the most astonishing relic of all – an immense obelisk made from 300 tons of Carrara marble, down the side of which, in bold capitals, are the words MUSSOLINI DUX.

How come all of this hasn't been demolished? It's a good question. One can find excuses. Mussolini wasn't nearly so bad as Hitler or Stalin (which is true, though he was pretty bad). After twenty years of Fascism, Romans were used to being surrounded by its emblems (also true). These were just another of the many historical layers of Rome, many of which had been built by emperors and popes who were quite as wicked as Mussolini (true again). Yet there's also another, less palatable reason why these souvenirs of dictatorship have survived. Many Romans feel nostalgia for the Fascist years. Behind us is the city's football stadium which, in October 2017, was plastered with anti-Semitic graffiti and images of Anne Frank wearing a Roma football shirt. On the other side of Rome there is a second great Fascist area, the suburb of EUR, which was originally intended to be a permanent exhibition of Fascism. Here one can find a large frieze depicting Italian achievements, in the centre of which is Mussolini riding a horse. At the end of the Second World War his nose was broken off, no doubt by some irate Roman, but a few years ago, when the city was governed by a right-wing mayor, Alemanno, it was quietly repaired.

Back we go, on the number 2 tram, into the centre of the city. This is the Via del Corso, one of Rome's main arteries, and a place long associated with cruelty. It's so long and straight that it looks relatively recent, but it's been here since classical times. During the Renaissance, races were held here during Carnival – the party days preceding Lent – between semi-naked Jews, and as they went by, crowds jeered and threw filth. Races were also run between young men, old men, donkeys, water buffaloes and – an innovation of the Borgia pope, Alexander VI – prostitutes. By the nineteenth century these contests had evolved into an equally brutal race by riderless horses. But there was also a charming silliness to Carnival at this time. In the daytime crowds of people, Romans and foreign visitors, poor and high-ranking, bombarded one another with posies of flowers and white plaster pellets that exploded over people's clothes. On the final evening of Carnival great battles were fought as everyone tried to douse everyone else's candle.

There, at the end of that crowded street, are the Spanish Steps. I know they're one of Rome's great sites, but if it's all right with you, I'd rather give them a miss, and the Trevi Fountain too, as they'll both be heaving with people. You can always go back another time. Instead, let's cut down to the right here, to the Piazza Sant'Ignazio, as there's a little game I'd like to play. It's a beautiful piazza and, with five lanes leading into it, it looks like an old theatre with numerous entrances through the scenery. In the 1790s, Rome's French revolutionary rulers had their offices here. There's something Parisian-looking about the buildings and perhaps it helped ease their homesickness. But it's the church of Sant'Ignazio that we've come to see. As we walk down the huge nave, do you notice anything a little strange? No? Still no? Yes, now you've got it. The dome at the far end of the church, that we've been looking up into, is no dome at all. The ceiling is as flat as a board and the whole thing is a clever *trompe l'œil*. Of course, it only works from certain viewpoints and now that we're underneath, the angles are absurdly exaggerated.

Back outside and down a narrow street we go, glimpsing a row of imposing classical columns up ahead, and here's Rome's most wonderful monument of all: the Pantheon. You already know all about it? The ingenious way the dome was constructed, using different mixes of concrete, that grow lighter as the dome becomes thinner and higher? That the whole glorious building is largely intact from when it was built, nineteen centuries ago? That it still has its original bronze doors, its original paving and even the original drainage system that carries away the rainwater that falls through the hole in the roof? You are well informed. But I bet you didn't know that the building also has an ancient mystery?

The Pantheon with its puzzling portico.

If you step back here, at the far end of the square, you can see how the triangular shape of the portico is echoed by a line of moulding above it. It could be an intentional design, of course, but once you start looking, it does seem odd. For that matter, the whole portico is wrongly proportioned – it seems too small for the rest of the building. And here's something else that's strange. Come over here beneath the portico. Do you see the two marble-covered pilasters to either side of the door? They're wide at the back but narrower at the front, so they're each shaped like a fat letter L. Amanda Claridge, author of *Rome: An Oxford Archaeological Guide*, has a theory about what all this means. She thinks the granite columns holding up the portico were supposed to be twelve Roman feet higher and much broader than they are. They were quarried in Egypt, and either something went badly wrong with the order, or the originals are somewhere at the bottom of the Mediterranean and these were all that could be found at short notice.

Now let's fight our way through the tour groups and cross the Corso del Rinascimento – another Mussolini demolition job – to one more of Rome's great sights: Piazza Navona. You know about this too? That's right, it follows the shape of a classical athletics stadium. It was built by Domitian, an unlikeable emperor – paranoid, murderous and also rather dull – though he nevertheless has a coffee bar over there named after him. Just outside the piazza to the north there's an excavated area where we can see remains of the original stadium (Mussolini again – he demolished the old houses that were above).

But I'll bet you didn't know that Jean-Paul Sartre and Simone de Beauvoir were here one evening in 1932. They'd come to Rome to mock Fascism and they soon found plenty of material. To their surprise they discovered that the city had no nightlife. Mussolini was determined to make his capital as drearily respectable as his hometown, Predappio in Emilia-Romagna, had been. Police and Fascist militiamen patrolled the streets and anyone who was still out after dinnertime would be moved on. If they showed disrespect they might even be sent into internal exile on one of the Fascist jail islands that dotted the Italian coast. Knowing that, as foreigners, they'd be safe from trouble, Sartre and de Beauvoir decided to provoke the regime and stay up till dawn. They sat talking in a deserted Piazza Navona until they were approached by two blackshirts who politely told them to go to bed. Unperturbed, they went on to the Colosseum where, at three in the morning, they were approached again, this time less politely, and reluctantly they went home to their hotel.

You're feeling a little tired? It's been quite a walk and Rome can be exhausting. But if you're up to it, there's one more place I'd like to look at, which I feel in some ways is as important as any other in the city. First, let's cross the busy Corso Vittorio Emanuele II. It's another main road that was driven through the fabric of the old city, though this one is pre-Mussolini and you can see the difference.

Rather than forcing its way through, straight and wide, it twists and weaves, so the finest buildings were preserved. Here's the Campo de' Fiori with its flower and food market. Perhaps we should get a little pizza to give us strength? In the far corner of the square to the right is some of the best takeaway pizza in Rome. My favourite is spicy chicory and pecorino cheese. And just over there is a wonderful example of how obstinately Rome resists the economic changes that have been sweeping the rest of the world. This is the most touristy market in Rome and many stalls now sell over-priced dried pasta and jars of condiments that no Roman would touch. Yet towards the south-east corner there's a stall that's run by a family from Velletri in the Alban Hills, who still grow their own produce. You won't find them here on Mondays or Thursdays as they're at home tending their fields, and everything they sell is wonderfully fresh and tasty. However, their prices are no higher than else-where. I swear their oranges are the best in Rome.

Here's the place I wanted you to see: the old Roman Ghetto. Although it is in fact misnamed, as the original ghetto, made up of tiny squares and cramped medieval slum housing, was demolished in the 1880s, replaced by apartment blocks and a large new synagogue. Romans, Jewish and Christian alike, were happy to see the back of it. Of course, if it had been cleaned up and preserved it would probably now be one of the city's most desirable neighbour-hoods – a Marais of Rome.

Somebody's waving. We're still remembered, though it's a dozen years since we lived here. Do you see the seven arched windows on the top floor of that building to the left? We were there for four years. It wasn't a huge flat and yet it seemed large, thanks to the airy space above, where the loft had been stripped out to reveal immense, worm-eaten beams. When we first moved in, we were regarded a little warily by our neighbours, but after we'd been here for a few months, and they realized we weren't just passing through, people were friendly and welcoming. Half the inhabitants of the neighbourhood are still Jewish and it's a tightly knit community – but you'd expect nothing else of a people with such a past. For three centuries they were forcibly segregated from Christian Romans in the walled ghetto, where they were locked in every night. During the day they were prohibited from any but the lowest and most demeaning work. Each Saturday they were required to go to a nearby church where a Christian priest lectured them on the wickedness of their beliefs (without success – hardly any of them converted).

Finally, let's cross the river, over the Ponte Fabricio, one of the oldest bridges on earth. It was built in 62 BC, the year after Cicero was consul, and when Julius Caesar was still an ambitious and little-known wannabe politician. Here's the Tiber Island where, in classical times, there was a famous temple to Asclepius, the god of healing, which, in Christian times, was replaced by a hospital. It's still there, still functioning, and

I've sat waiting in its accident and emergency area following several minor mishaps in our family.

In 1943 there was also a tobacconist's kiosk on this spot and, as cigarettes were hard to come by, very early on the morning of the 16th of October that year, a number of Jewish men from the ghetto came here and joined the queue, waiting for the kiosk to open. As they waited, German troops sealed off the ghetto behind them. They were not the only lucky ones that day. Some inhabitants of the ghetto were allowed to slip away by unfanatical German soldiers who'd been charmed by a gift of cigarettes, while a number of Jewish men managed to escape over the rooftops. Their wives, who assumed the Germans were seeking forced labour and wouldn't be interested in them or their children, stayed behind – but of course they were mistaken. Of the thousand and more Jewish Romans taken from the ghetto that morning, most of whom were women and children, only fifteen returned alive.

Back we go to Trastevere and we're almost home. I know, there's an awful lot we missed. We didn't see the Colosseum or the Forum or the Palatine Hill, nor the piazza on the Capitoline Hill that was beautifully designed by Michelangelo, let alone the Lateran area, or the many sights around Termini station. I forgot to point out any of the medieval towers – there are plenty of them, still – which were once so numerous that the city was quite a porcupine. We didn't see a single one of the city's early churches, some of which are beautifully preserved, nor did we go into any of Rome's wonderful museums. And there's much more I would have liked to tell you about: Rome's emperors and popes – innocents and monsters – the artists who were here, and the many writers who came to visit. Nor did I say anything about the Roman Resistance during the Nazi occupation, which was the most formidable partisan group in Italy during the war. But then you can't expect to get to know all of Rome in one day.

What's that? There was rather a lot about Mussolini and Fascism? That's true I know, but I feel that it's important to remember that time, especially now, when the world is drifting back in that direction. I'm amazed that anyone can be persuaded by the ninety-year-old propaganda of a failed regime and believe that Mussolini was a capable leader. Judged by the two measures that Fascism held most dear – economic growth and war – his regime was a disastrous failure. Under Fascism the Italian economy was among the slowest growing in Europe. Mussolini sneered at the liberal democracy that preceded his rule, despising it as inefficient and corrupt, yet Fascism was far more crooked. Under democratic rule Italy's economic growth had outpaced Germany's, and in the First World War the armies of Italy's elected government fought bravely and – for a poor country struggling against far richer ones – did well.

Italian disasters in the Second World War are well known. Less well known is that Mussolini had poured money into his military and, thanks to government incompetence, it vanished into the sand. Italians drove tanks that were so tiny and useless they were nicknamed 'sardine cans' and Italian pilots flew bombers whose engines would overheat and burst into flames. Mussolini himself was half the problem. He led Italians into a war they never believed in and then, convinced by his own propaganda, decided he was a military genius and refused to consult his generals, instead directing the war himself, only to keep changing his mind. One moment he planned to invade Croatia, next it was Greece, then it was North Africa. When he finally attacked the British in Egypt, he'd sent all his trucks to the Croatian frontier, and an immense Italian army had to walk across the desert. It was no surprise that everything went wrong.

I'm sorry, I'm going on again. It's because I feel so passionately about this. Can't people see? Dictators tell us they get things done but dictatorship is the most inefficient form of government. If it seems to work today you can be sure it won't work tomorrow. The only way people can hope to be governed tolerably well is to watch their rulers like hawks, regard everything they say as a lie and, when they become sleepy and crooked – as they inevitably will – fling them out and replace them with others who aren't yet drunk on their power.

Now, here we are, by the Education Ministry building that marks the edge of my lockdown bubble. And I have to say, I do feel a little freer for having had this walk around the city with you today, even if it was only in my thoughts.

Spring is here – and a recipe for *Pasta alla vignarola*

Very tentatively – and rightly so – the Italian government is beginning to loosen things a little. Last Monday
Shannon was surprised to see a woman walking down Viale
Trastevere carrying a pot plant. Our local garden centre has
been allowed to reopen. Shannon seized her chance, paid
several visits and planted new flowers on our balcony, and
they look beautiful. The sight of them outside the windows
is very cheering. The Lazio authorities have announced that
after Easter art-supply shops and bookshops will reopen,
though customers will have to wear gloves and a mask. It's
a sensible move that will help both sectors keep going and
will give people more to do in their locked-down lives.

Tatiana may be an early customer at the art shops. Now
that Easter is here and her online lessons have stopped,
she's dug out an old easel and has been drawing and painting. Alexander will have even more time on his hands. His
final school IB exams were cancelled a couple of weeks
ago. Last week he took two maths tests organized by the
school to help them estimate grades, and now all he has left
to do is wait for the IB to produce his final results, which

are to be calculated in a fiendishly complicated way using students' course work, school predictions and world data – whatever that is. I hope everything will work out all right for him. But then who doesn't have uncertainties right now, and far graver ones than ours? (Makers of gloves and surgical masks – that's who.)

Spring is here. Usually at Easter it pours with rain, drenching the crowds who fill St Peter's Square and spoiling Romans' getaway plans, but this year, when nobody can get away anywhere, the weather taunts us and remains beautiful, day after day. This morning, when I went for my walk round our bubble, I felt a definite change. The sun had a sense of warning, a hint of what it can and will do in a couple of months. Six weeks ago, when the virus was nothing more than a threat from the north, it occurred to me that I should buy some shorts, but of course back then there were none to be found. I'm sure I have a couple of pairs somewhere, a little ragged, but they'll do.

Seeing as yesterday's entry was so very long, I feel this will suffice for today. As spring is here, I'll finish with a recipe for the definitive springtime pasta: *alla vignarola* (which roughly translates as 'pasta greengrocer style'). I first had it in a small restaurant in the Maremma area – the nearest and least fashionable part of Tuscany – and it was so good that I had to try reproducing it myself. It's not a precise recipe and nobody will judge you harshly if you use a slightly different combination of spring vegetables, so long as it all tastes good in the end. Likewise, you can vary the quantities. This is on the generous side.

Pasta alla vignarola

Serves four as a main course

Ingredients:

1 white onion, chopped

30ml olive oil

1 stalk of celery, chopped

2 spring onions, chopped

Pancetta – one thick chunk per person, chopped into cubes

500g pasta – I use a large tube such as rigatoni though some recipes advise fusilli

Black pepper

1 cup of dry white wine

200g broad beans, freshly shelled

A dozen asparagus spears, broken or chopped so the parts aren't too big – fairly thin ones for preference, with the inedible bottom parts removed

200g peas, freshly shelled

4 artichoke hearts – Romans use different artichokes from the northern countries and it's a lot of work to prepare them, so it's not shameful to use some from a jar

Butter

Salt and pepper

A few sprigs of basil – the Romans use a north African

mint, mentuccia, but basil is fine

Pecorino Romano

Method:

Set the water boiling for the pasta.

Fry the onion in olive oil till it's yellow and soft. Add the celery and spring onion till they're cooked. Remove the vegetable mix from the pan and set aside for now.

Fry the pancetta till nicely done.

Once the water's boiling, add the pasta.

Return the fried onion and celery to the pan with the pancetta and season with a couple of twists of black pepper.

Pour in the white wine and use it to boil the vegetables. Start with the broad beans as they'll take longer, then add the asparagus and peas. If you're using artichoke from a jar, that will need hardly any time. You don't need much liquid. If the sauce is going dry, ladle in a little water from the pasta.

When it's ready, a little butter added will do no harm. Add pepper and salt to taste.

Mix the sauce with the cooked pasta, throw on the basil leaves and serve, with plenty of grated Pecorino Romano cheese on the side for people to add.

Mysteries, conspiracies and the shooting of Sister Piera

It's Easter Sunday. Today, Pope Francis celebrated Easter Mass in an all but deserted Saint Peter's. We didn't watch it on television as we stare at screens quite enough at the moment. During the day we all work on computers and in the evening we've been watching classic films. Last night it was Ridley Scott's *Alien*. Four decades on, I was surprised by how good it looked. The visuals were still remarkable and there were some highly disturbing scenes. The only moment when the film really showed its age was when Sigourney Weaver consulted the ship's computer, 'Mother', which appeared to be a vast Amstrad in a roomful of flashing lights.

Alien was all the more disturbing as it seems strangely pertinent. The crew of the *Nostromo* just can't overcome a pesky intruder that's constantly changing and is impossible to find or see until it's too late. How very familiar. The latest figure for new coronavirus infections in Italy, which had been falling steadily, has begun rising again. There's probably an explanation but it is still discouraging. Last night I read that in South Korea fifty-one people who had recovered from the disease went on to test positive for a second time. It's unclear if they were re-infected or if the virus had staged a revival within them. News of this kind makes one wonder if we'll ever be free of this plague.

As at any time when a mysterious new disease strikes, there are conspiracy theories, some of which have been given greater credence via endorsements by nationalist populist politicians. Was coronavirus engineered in a Chinese bio-warfare lab? Or in an American bio-warfare lab? Or there's the bizarre claim by former BBC television presenter and noted conspiracy theorist David Icke that coronavirus has been deliberately spread from 5G masts. Icke also maintains that when a vaccination eventually appears it will contain a tiny microchip to control people's minds. Such a notion would be entirely laughable except that in the UK – a country I always felt was more rational than most – it has led people in Birmingham and Merseyside to burn down 5G masts. As has been pointed out in the British press, such vandalism will make it harder for health workers to communicate and fight the virus.

Over here, surveys have shown that more than a quarter of Italians believe the coronavirus wasn't a natural occurrence but was the result of a foreign plot. This doesn't greatly surprise me. In my experience Italians have an openness to conspiracy theories, and when any matter is discussed, from football to politics, I often hear claims of secret scheming. In part, I suspect, conspiracies seem plausible here because things are often not as clear-cut as they are in northern countries.

If that sounds like a terrible generalization, I'll offer an example: New Year's Eve. In the past we've sometimes climbed the Gianicolo Hill just above us to celebrate, as it's a good place from which to watch fireworks being let off all across the city. It's crowded with clusters of people, each with a bottle of prosecco and wine glasses. I've watched as a nearby group counts from ten down to zero and there's a cheer and the clinking of glasses. The New Year has arrived. But has it? Now another group does exactly the same thing, and then several other groups do so, too. Each has been guided by somebody's watch that's set slightly differently from the others. The roar of fireworks is no help as it's been going on for ages and will continue for long afterwards. In a northern country I feel there would be more of a need for an absolute moment of New Year, agreed by all. In Rome nobody's too bothered. For each group, their own relative New Year's moment is quite good enough. It's the same with Roman clocks. If my watch isn't working, time becomes a mystery. Viale Trastevere near our flat is lined with clocks but no two show the same hour. Some are still in winter time, others are simply wrong and some have stopped altogether. With careful study one can learn which are the most accurate but there's no guarantee that they'll remain so.

Lack of clarity can affect larger matters, too. Our journalist friend, Barbie, covered the infamous Meredith

Kercher murder trial and wrote a book about it, *Angel Face: The True Story of Student Killer Amanda Knox*. Whenever we met, she'd give us all the latest news, so I felt I knew every last detail, yet to this day it's still anything but clear. Of the three defendants, one, Rudy Guede, opted for a fast-track trial which meant he never had to testify. The other two, Amanda Knox and Raffaele Sollecito, were found guilty and then, at a higher court, not guilty, then guilty again and they were finally acquitted. In all the trials and retrials, and through the many millions of words written about the case, the one thing that has never emerged with any clarity is who did what and why?

Obscurity and conspiracies are a constant feature of Italian politics. In 1978 Aldo Moro, Christian Democrat leader and two-time Prime Minister of Italy, was found in the boot of a car on Via Caetani beside the Roman Ghetto. He'd been kidnapped, held hostage and eventually murdered by the leftist revolutionary terror group the Brigate Rosse (the Red Brigades). That much is clearly known, yet to this day uncertainty surrounds the case. Was he abandoned to his fate by his fellow Christian Democrats for being too conciliatory towards the Italian Communist Party? Was his killing ordered by the US government to conceal their interference in Italy?

An equally thick fog hangs over one of the more bizarre moments in Italian post-war politics: the coup attempt of

7 December 1970. At the height of the Cold War a group of neo-fascists set out to occupy Rome's television centre and other key installations so their leader, Prince Junio Borghese, could announce he had seized control of the country. To this day nobody knows why the coup was aborted, though a faulty lift may have played a role. Four months passed before anyone noticed it had even been attempted. Decades of prosecutions ended without any lasting guilty verdicts of note, and some still insist that the coup never happened at all.

We have a curious local mystery here in Trastevere. In late April 2001, shortly before we moved here, local newspapers reported that a 62-year-old nun, Sister Piera, had been shot while walking on the Viale Trastevere, just a kilometre or so south of our present bubble. She was part of the order of the Francescane del Verbo Incarnato (Franciscan sisters of the Holy Word in Mortal Form) who had a small convent nearby on Via Traversari. Newspapers reported that Sister Piera heard a bang and then felt a pain in her shoulder. She didn't understand what had happened until people on the street pointed out to her that she was bleeding. She managed to return to the convent and was then taken to a nearby hospital, where she was treated – fortunately her injury was not life-threatening. Others in the convent reported that Sister Piera had no enemies and was well liked. Initial police investigations suggested she had been shot from a window above her.

Who would shoot a nun walking down the road? The case soon became more puzzling still. Comparisons were quickly made with another shooting, four years earlier, of a university student, Marta Russo, who was killed when walking with a friend in the grounds of La Sapienza University. But, in this highly controversial case, which was never clearly resolved, the accused was already in prison.

To further muddy the waters of Sister Piera's case, the initial account given by the convent was then called into question. The police could find no traces of blood on the Viale Trastevere, where Sister Piera was supposed to have been shot, nor could they find any members of the public who'd seen her there, though there should have been plenty of witnesses, as the incident took place at midday on a Sunday, when the area is crowded with people going to the nearby Porta Portese flea market. Strangest of all, burn marks on Sister Piera's habit indicated that the gun had been fired from close range, around fifty centimetres away. The newspapers conjectured that the shooting must have actually taken place inside the convent.

After twelve months, during which time no evidence was found to indicate any suspect, the police investigation was abandoned. Then, a dozen years later, it reappeared in Rome's press, when journalists questioned whether the case might be connected with two other mysterious pistol shootings in the area (which was now referred to, dramatically, as 'The Triangle of Blood'). Late one night in

February 1999, two years before the shooting of Sister Piera, a private investigator had been shot on a deserted platform of Ostiense railway station. And in February 2013 – a dozen years after the attack on Sister Piera – a celebrity photographer was found shot dead by Testaccio Bridge. Today, the fog surrounding Sister Piera's case shows no sign of dispersing.

Among Rome's greatest mysteries is a very ancient one that concerns the city's very *raison d'être*. The papacy's claim for primacy within the Catholic Church has always rested on its contention that a direct line of succession could be traced from the reigning pope right back to Jesus, via Saint Peter, who was Jesus' disciple, his anointed successor and Rome's first bishop. Yet it is highly questionable that Peter ever came to Rome. Without getting too bogged down in early Christian history, I should explain that Saint Paul – who never met Jesus – was the one who changed the direction of Jesus' movement and took it westwards, when he began converting non-Jews, who proved far more receptive to Jesus' notions than the Jews had been. There is no evidence that Jesus' old guard of disciples in Jerusalem – including Peter – had any interest in converting non-Jews, or travelled anywhere, let alone to Rome.

But what about the body? According to Christian tradition, Peter died in Rome in the time of Emperor Nero. He was crucified in Nero's Gardens and buried nearby, on the slopes of the Vatican Hill. Three centuries later, when Emperor Constantine proclaimed the Roman Empire was Christian, and began construction of the first Saint Peter's Basilica, it was built so that Saint Peter's remains lay directly beneath the altar. During the Second World War the pro-Nazi pope, Pius XII, had a German churchman, Ludwig Kaas, excavate the ancient cemetery beneath St Peter's, and Kaas duly found a plain tomb monument directly beneath the altar, yet his discovery brought more questions than answers. Among the graffiti scratched into the walls, Peter's name was written only once (Christian martyrs in tombs beneath other Rome churches were recorded dozens of times). More puzzlingly, the bones in the grave, which belonged to a man in his sixties, appeared to date from the time not of Emperor Nero, when Peter was supposed to have died, but of Emperor Vespasian, who ruled a decade later. Neither Pius nor Kaas were happy with the finds and for some time the bones went missing.

It seems the claim that Saint Peter was Rome's first bishop may well have been a sleight of hand by early Christian Romans, eager to make their city the capital of Christianity as well as of the Roman Empire. If so, their deceit was a dazzlingly successful one, which would be the making of the papacy and Rome. And I can't say I have a problem with the thought that the Rome I know and love may have been built on the back of a vast lie. I'm just happy it exists.

Daring to look to the future: Rome in four seasons

Last night, the number of deaths and new infections were both down, which is encouraging, and the Italian government issued new details on relaxing the lockdown. Tomorrow, bookshops and stationery shops will reopen, subject to the usual social distancing restrictions. In three weeks' time, if the numbers continue to fall, there will be free movement once again, though people will have to wear masks and practise social distancing. It seems that, finally, the end of our bubble life is in sight. I'll be able to cross the river once again and make sure the Pantheon's still there. On that same day clothing shops will reopen, so I'll even be able to buy some shorts. Two weeks' later, bars and restaurants will reopen, so we might manage a pizza at Da Ivo. And a week after that, on the 25th, I'll even be able to get my hair cut – though I imagine there'll be quite a queue.

Yet the government doesn't expect the crisis to be over – far from it. Sports competitions should restart on the last day of May, but schools will stay shut until September, and even then some may continue with online lessons. Cinemas and theatres won't open till December. There will be restrictions on people entering Italy from countries that still have problems with the virus. A full end to restrictions is predicted only for the 31st of March 2021. Though, of course, at this stage that's nothing more than wishful thinking.

It's extraordinary how much our view of the world is dictated by government rulings. Though I ceased to make any long-term plans in January, it was only when the lockdown was declared across Italy five weeks ago, that I truly grasped the urgency of the situation. Likewise, it's only now, with this new government statement, that I find myself beginning to look to the future once more. Now, I can start thinking about the problem that is summer.

I should explain a little about the seasons in Rome as, for anyone who lives in a cool, northern country, they're curiously inverted. Autumn and winter, which are the two seasons I like the least in the UK, I look forward to here. Autumn in Rome is dramatic. Flocks of starlings appear on their way south to Africa, forming immense shifting shapes in the skies above the city centre, and then drop down into trees that they fill in such numbers that it's hard to see how they can possibly fit. They also shit so abundantly that, whatever the weather, prudent Romans won't venture out without an umbrella. City employees in white protective suits are sent out with megaphones to play taped cries of predator birds in an attempt to scare the birds away, but they never seem too troubled.

Autumn isn't usually cold here. The centralized heating system in our apartment block isn't scheduled to come on till mid-November, though if an icy wind descends residents can sign a form that Cinzia keeps in her kiosk, and request it to be switched on earlier. As the days are short, autumn is a warm, dark season. Most of all, it's a time of thunderstorms. If you're unlucky enough to be caught out in one without the right gear, you can be drenched to the skin in a matter of moments. Thunderstorms can also cause serious damage. There have been a good many times when I've jumped out of bed in the small hours of the night and hurried round the flat, disconnecting electrical items as the roars of thunder grow louder.

A strong storm can turn our road, which weaves down the Gianicolo Hill, into a river. Ten years ago a particularly bad one flooded underpasses across Rome and sent cars floating away. It also inundated our apartment block's heating system beneath the courtyard, destroying it. Another memorable deluge came one afternoon when I was driving Tatiana back from visiting friends who lived by the sea. Roads back into the city closed before me, one after the other, so I was diverted ever farther round the clockface of the city's ring road, waved on by police so drenched that I saw two of them laughing and taking selfies.

But if autumn weather is mixed, it's a good time for food. Summer is a relatively lean time for eating in Rome – the land's too parched – but by the third week of September market stalls become filled with new produce. This includes two delicious citrus fruits, both of which have dark green skins but are orange inside. One is the mapo, a mildly sour blend of grapefruit and mandarins, and the other – my favourite – is the miyagawa, an oriental fruit that's like a less sweet version of a satsuma. But you have to enjoy them both while you can, as within a month their season is over and they're gone. As they disappear, the first oranges arrive: small, greenish-skinned and sour, though they soon grow sweeter. Then numerous kinds of grapes can be found, including uva fragola – strawberry grapes – which really do taste like strawberries. Among the autumn vegetables, a couple are distinctively Roman. Agretti, which has a rich flavour, looks like a mop of dark green hair and one could imagine finding it washed up on a beach. Puntarelle is a variety of chicory, but from which the leaves are discarded and only the thin, slightly bitter stalks are consumed. They're eaten raw as a salad, and are delicious with a dressing of oil, garlic, lemon and mashed anchovies.

And of course, there's that favourite of Romans, the artichoke, which fills market stalls from autumn to spring. In Italy these come in different varieties from those found in northern European countries, and are smaller with purple outer leaves. The Roman way of cooking them is quite different, too. The hard work is in their preparation: removing the inedible outer leaves, peeling off the hard edge of the stalk and scraping out the choke with a spoon, till everything that remains is edible. Then they're either deep fried, *alla Giudia* (Jewish-style), till they're brown and crispy with soft green parts inside, or they're slow cooked in a pot, *alla Romana* (Roman-style), with olive oil, garlic, lemon juice and a north African mint, mentuccia. Either way, they're well worth the effort.

In early December, the storms usually come to an end, the skies clear and winter begins. It's one of my favourite seasons here. There may be a few miserable, chilly days but there will also be plenty that are bright, with a wonderful white light that seems to glow. Even in January, if the sun's shining one can sit in suntrap restaurants where people have lunch outside wearing only shirts – at least until the sun drops behind a building, cold suddenly descends and everyone hurries to put on every layer of clothing they have.

And, if you're very lucky indeed, you might witness something quite extraordinary. When we first moved to Rome one of my dreams was to see the city under snow. I knew it was unlikely, as it had last snowed here in 1986, but in February 2012, after ten years of waiting, my dream came true. I got up at five in the morning when the snow was freshly fallen and walked across the city, amazed at how wonderful it looked. It was a different Rome, with a different colour scheme: orange and white. And then, six years later, it happened again. Shannon was away at a conference but I managed to persuade Alexander and Tatiana to get up with me at five, and for several hours we walked through the falling snow. It was the strangest feeling. It was as if I'd made a journey back to a place that I knew well but that was exceptionally hard to reach.

The Vittoriano in a rare blizzard.

By late February one can already feel the sun growing warm. Despite suffering from hay fever, I love the spring. But then, who doesn't? The evenings are long, the colours are bright. In May, creepers burst into dazzling purple and orange flowers – if I were a better man, I'd be able to tell you what they are. Tomatoes, which are a little lacklustre in mid-winter, regain their tang. The markets become filled with plums, apricots, peaches, tabbacchieri (literally 'tobacco pouches' – the Italian name for flat peaches), melons, watermelons, and also fruits that rarely reach northern countries, such as nespole, which are crunchy, sweet and a little bitter.

The only season I don't look forward to is summer. It's a great time of year if you're in the mountains or by the sea, but in Rome it's too much. Around the summer solstice the temperature often jumps up from 30 to 36 and Romans wilt. If it's 38 or higher you know, because when you breathe in, the air feels hot in your mouth – hotter than you are. You might think Romans would be used to the heat but no, they moan and complain, just as the English moan about damp, lightless winter days, and Ontarians complain about the cold.

The Romans have ways to make their summers more bearable. The streets are quiet in the afternoon when the heat is at its worst, but in the late evening the city becomes crowded with families going out for some air. A favourite spot is not far from our flat, on the Gianicolo Hill, by the equestrian statue of Garibaldi, where there's often a slight cooling breeze. People can enjoy the view of the floodlit city below, have a drink from one of the kiosks, and listen to live music at a cocktail bar that's set up there each summer. A little farther along there's an open-air theatre, with stone seats curved into the hillside, where a company that specializes in Plautus comedies performs. We've only been once but it was a memorable experience. We sat in the back row, where you could see the skyline of Rome rising up behind the stage, though that night the real drama was in the audience. One of the cast had been married that same day and his American bride sat watching in the audience in her wedding dress, surrounded by her family and guests. Whenever one of the actors had a line that was suggestively pertinent to wedding nights, they'd deliver it directly to her. She took it all very well.

The other place for hot Romans to cool down is the Tiber. For most of the year the river embankments are empty, aside from runners, cyclists and homeless people camped out under bridges, but from mid-June a great transformation begins. Wooden structures rise up that then grow into shops, bars and restaurants. On the Tiber Island there's an open-air cinema. The whole area is lit with coloured lights and is kept beautifully cool by the river rushing by – natural air conditioning.

Despite such wonders, most Romans choose to escape. July, which is often the hottest month, is still a working time, and the roads are crowded with drivers looking angry and scorched in their cars, but at the beginning of August everything goes quiet. It's a strange month, and has a special, moody atmosphere. For the first two weeks you find yourself walking ever farther to find a bar that's still open and will give you a coffee and cornetto. If you go to the same bar three times running you may find yourself welcomed like an old friend – as Romans feel more alone and are hungry for company, they become friendlier and the city feels like a small Italian town. And, with hardly a car on the roads, the air grows cleaner. Quietness reaches its climax on the 15th of August, the Ferragosto national holiday. If you break an arm then, your best hope of finding a doctor is probably to race to the coast and shout 'Is there a doctor on the beach?'

Of course, Roman summers are not all the same. Some are merely hot, with the temperature rarely topping 31 or 32, and with delightful warm evenings. Others are hard to endure. By chance, I was here for almost the whole of the summer of 2003, when all of Europe baked and thousands of elderly people died in Paris from the heat (few died in Rome – their families were more watchful). That year the temperature reached the thirties in late April and remained there, with hardly a break, until September. I remember that summer as a dark time because I lived in dim rooms with shutters closed to keep out the scalding sunlight. As I like to go for a walk each day, from late afternoon I'd open a window from time to time, to test when the air felt cooler outside than in. I sometimes had to wait till 10.30 at night and when I got back from walking I'd be drenched in sweat. Since that year we've tried to avoid being in Rome for too much of the summer. We visit relatives in Canada or the UK, or we arrange house swaps, which have taken us to all kinds of interesting places.

And this summer? Like everyone else, we'll wait and see.

A down day – and a recipe for comfort pasta

The rollercoaster rumbles on. Yesterday I was up, excited by the government's schedule for relaxing the lockdown, but then in the evening our journalist friend, Barbie, passed on a piece she'd written for the *Daily Beast*, about an Italian newsreader, Alessandro Politi. After a work colleague came down with the virus, Politi, who'd had nothing more than a slight sore throat, was tested and was surprised to find he was positive. Two weeks later he tested positive again, as he did after another week, and yet again after thirty days. Whether he was infectious all this time is anybody's guess, but the Lombardy government is taking no chances and has just doubled the self-quarantine required of anyone with symptoms, from fourteen to twenty-eight days.

Once again, it's clear this is going to be a long process and a very destructive one. Some restaurants in Rome have already announced they're closing down for good. Even if they're allowed to reopen next month, with social distancing they'll find it hard to fit in enough customers to make ends meet. And that's just the restaurants. Any real hope lies with a vaccine and that clearly isn't going to appear any time soon, if it ever does. To top it all, last night we started watching the TV series *Chernobyl*. It wasn't a wise choice: a disaster whose effects spread rapidly across borders, people vomiting up blood, an invisible foe, blinkered authorities in denial. I went to bed with a racing heart. Tonight, we'll pick something a little lighter, like *Singing in the Rain*.

I'll end this short entry with a pasta sauce recipe. I can't claim this to be Roman, or even Italian, as I invented it myself. We call it comfort pasta and we eat it when we're feeling in need of reassurance – like today. It's not healthy in any way, and should be consumed with the greatest of care and only by people with no medical conditions of any kind. But here it is.

Comfort Pasta

Serves four

Ingredients:

One whole head of garlic, chopped

Half a chilli pepper

Pancetta bacon – one thick strip per person, cut into small cubes

Dry white wine – at least a cup

Most of a 280g jar of sundried tomatoes, chopped

500g pasta, any kind of large tube (rigatoni, tortiglioni)

400g (approx.) spring peas (frozen is fine)

200ml single cream

Parmesan and pecorino cheese – lots

Method:

Set the water boiling for the pasta.

Fry the garlic and the chilli pepper, remove from the pan and set aside for now.

Cook the bacon, adding wine to stop it from burning.

When the bacon's cooked, add the sundried tomatoes and also the garlic and chilli pepper that you removed from the pan earlier. Lightly cook and, as before, add wine to stop it from burning.

Start boiling the pasta.

Add the peas to the sauce. You can add them frozen as they'll soon heat up.

When the peas are cooked, add the cream and cook till it's thickened. If the sauce looks like it's going too dry, add a little water from the cooking pasta. It's good with a little liquid, not too much.

When the pasta's cooked, mix with the sauce and serve with pecorino and parmesan on the side.

Is it a lie that Romans are friendly?

This morning I went to the market with our wheelie trolley for the weekly shop. It was another fine day and, as I passed through the market piazza, I looked uneasily at two old men sitting chatting on a bench. Was that a metre between them? It looked like less. Initially the Italian government proposed that everyone should keep two metres apart from each other – the distance required in many other countries – but following resistance it was reduced to one: a poor compromise, I suspect.

But then what can you do? Italians are an emotionally unrestrained, warm-hearted people and that just can't be changed. As I write these words, I feel an alarm bell sound within me. I've just repeated a long-established cliché that has appeared over the years in endless books and films, and it's one that many here find highly irritating. Shannon's Italian colleagues are regularly driven into social media rage when some eminent foreign Italophile praises Rome as a city of smiling, golden-hearted angels. They've bought the bullshit, Shannon's colleagues fume. How can they be so blind? Can't they see that Romans are the very opposite: tough, stingy, calculating and, above all, selfish.

But that can't be true, the Romaphiles will answer. Romans are so welcoming. And it's true that it's easy to feel accepted here. Romans come across as uncomplicated towards foreigners in a way few other peoples are. In general most of them don't seem greatly bothered that you're living in their city. Of course, they're used to foreign visitors. They've had seventeen centuries of pilgrims and three centuries of sightseers. For that matter, there have been times when the majority of Romans came from somewhere else. A large portion of the population of classical Rome consisted of immigrants, both slaves and free. During the Renaissance, when Rome was a boom town, half of all Romans came from elsewhere in Italy and a fifth from another part of Europe altogether. It's been the same in more recent times. In the last century and a half there has been a constant influx of people from nearby regions of Italy – many have their own clubs here – and in recent decades these have been joined by Eastern Europeans, people from the Philippines, Brazil, Peru, Bangladesh and, more recently, from Afghanistan, the Middle East and sub-Saharan Africa.

Sadly, if Romans are easy-going towards white northerners, that doesn't mean they're welcoming towards everyone. While some Romans treat overseas employees well, others are high-handed, exploitative and miserly. When going about Rome I've seen how aloof many Romans are towards immigrants from Africa and Asia. It's become noticeably worse in recent years with the rise of the Lega party. The party's leader, Matteo Salvini, like nationalist populists across the world has, in some Romans' minds, made racism seem almost respectable. I've seen a couple of ugly incidents in the last year, in both of which an immigrant was abused, mostly verbally but also physically, by a middle-aged Roman with a shaved head. Since the financial crisis of 2008 one can see the frustration on people's faces, and now a major political figure is offering them an easy target at which to vent their anger. When the coronavirus began its spread in Italy, Salvini was quick to insist that Italy must be protected from incomers, in particular Chinese and also Africans, even though at this point the virus had barely arrived in Africa. A number of Chinese were physically attacked, together with other individuals from East Asia who were mistaken for Chinese.

Yet, I've also seen Romans who have treated immigrants with conspicuous kindness and have accepted them with the same easy-going, first-name friendliness that they show to one another. Like everything else here, it's personal. Yet the fact that the personal is key here can work against new arrivals. This is a city where connections are everything and it's hard for an outsider to break through. It's the same for northerners, who struggle to find any employment that doesn't rely on their foreignness: working for an international agency like the United Nations Food and Agriculture Organization, teaching English as a foreign language, working as a journalist for foreign outlets or, for that matter, writing books about Rome for foreign readers. Rome is a very different city from Berlin, London or Toronto, where new arrivals have a real opportunity to thrive. Immigrants here know that this is the case and most of those who have fought their way to Italy from Africa or Asia have little desire to stay. If they can, they move on to northern Europe.

So we can accept that the Romans aren't perfect, and some can be racist, yet there's no denying their warmth and emotionality. Or is there? A colleague and close friend of Shannon's, Alessandra, is in an especially good position to offer enlightenment here, as she has a foot in two cultures. Her father was Jewish Roman, born in the Roman Ghetto and a very lucky survivor of the Nazi sweep of October 1943 – he was a newborn and so tiny that the German soldiers didn't find him (his mother, hiding in an attic, saw her mother being dragged away, holding a bundle and thought, mistakenly, that it was her son). Alessandra's mother, by contrast, is from an Anglo-Welsh family. Once, when talking about her childhood, Alessandra told me something that I've never forgotten. She said that as a child she always liked to visit her British relatives because, compared with her Roman relations, they were eccentric (many had led colourful lives in the British Empire) and also they were more emotional. The repressed English are more emotional than the passionate Italians? What on earth's going on?

At the real risk of making a fool of myself with a dose of national stereotyping, I think I need to give this matter some consideration. It's undeniable that Romans, including Jewish Romans, can be tough. It's no surprise considering what they've endured over the centuries. I've already related a little of what Jewish Romans have experienced during the last five hundred years, and it hasn't been easy for Christian Romans either. Their city has been through horrific sackings, massacres, rule by French revolutionaries, by a papal police state, by a Fascist police state, and it's inhabitants suffered near-starvation under Nazi occupiers. Few visitors realize it, as the city centre came through largely unscathed, but Rome also endured its own blitz by Allied bombers, and it was a bad one too, with an estimated 7,000 Romans killed.

I suspect the answer, as far as there is one, lies in the fact that Romans are better at connecting with one another than northern peoples. They're also informal. They'll greet you on the street whether they know you very well or only slightly. They're quick to remember one another's first names and will use these on every occasion, often shortened for greater familiarity. Friendliness from a stranger, which is often met with some suspicion in the Anglo-Saxon world – why is this person being so friendly, what do they want? – is rarely rebuffed here. It's seen as good manners, while coolness will be answered in kind. Of course, the fact that somebody knows your name doesn't mean they'll tell you their innermost secrets, or listen to your woes, or feed your cat when you're away, or help you move flat. Though who knows, they might do all of these things.

To throw another gross generalization into the mix, I would say that, alongside the selfishness that many Romans are capable of, you will also usually find, if you look hard enough, a strong sense of humanity. Roman drivers are rarely celebrated for their forbearance, and yet they will show surprising patience when stuck behind a slow-moving learner driver. Likewise, they're tolerant when two cars stop in front of them, blocking the whole road, and one driver asks directions of the other. In both cases there is need and vulnerability, and compassion should be shown.

Education says much about a people, and though our children have mostly studied at international schools here, we have some knowledge of the Italian system too. Tatiana went to an Italian Catholic school for a year and both children followed the Italian curriculum and took Italian state exams until they were fourteen. Education in Rome is functional and tough. The Roman state schools I've seen are cramped, crowded and lacking any outside areas aside from a courtyard. Since the 2008 crisis they're also often rundown. In the UK many people have been angered by the savage effect of cuts, and rightly so, but they would be shocked by how few extras one finds here when it comes to music or art or sports. If a Roman child dreams of playing football for Roma or taking their place on the Italian Olympic team or playing first violin in an orchestra, it's up to the parents to get them started at a sports association or with music lessons. Yet academic standards are often high. Our children moved between studying maths in the International and the Italian systems, and they found Italian maths lessons were always more rigorous and the level was more advanced. That said, the teaching in Italian schools is often ungenerous. There's little spoon-feeding, students are expected to find their own way and at the best high schools it's assumed that a good number of students will fail to keep up, and will drop out and move to somewhere less demanding. And yet, even in Rome's tough education system one can find a strong vein of humanity. During a school exam, if a student seeks a little help from another and this is given, it's unlikely to be regarded with the strong disapproval that it would meet with in a northern country. Showing charity to those in need is commendable.

Many Italian school exams are oral and rather terrifying. I accompanied both our children when they took the standard, state, end of middle school exam for fourteen-year-olds – the *terza media* – and saw the intimidating panel of teachers, ranged behind a long desk as they shot forth questions. A student who was interrogated before Alexander had learning difficulties, and in another country I suspect he might have been placed in a specialist school. I felt nervous for him but I needn't have. The panel showed him the utmost patience and gently helped him to find his way through the process. Results were announced instantly and when he heard he had passed, and with a respectable mark, he was joyful in a way I've rarely witnessed, as were his family and friends. As to how rigorous the grading had been, that I couldn't say (and I doubt he would have been treated so gently at the end of high school, which is tougher), yet the humanity of the moment was wonderful to see.

In Rome humanity is seldom far away. A while back a ginger cat began hanging around the entrance area to our building and our *portiera*, Cinzia, would regularly complain about what a lazy, useless animal it was, forever pestering her. After a while, though her grumbles continued, I saw it sitting with her in the kiosk. Later I spotted her discreetly giving it food and then amusing it with cat toys she'd bought. Likewise, she sometimes complains about the behaviour of people in our building – and with good reason, as a few of them are quite monstrous – yet she looks after everybody. She's swapped telephone numbers with the Poste Italiane girl and the delivery people, so she doesn't miss anyone's packages. There's an elderly woman on our stairway who is largely blind and deaf, and I've seen Cinzia, early in the morning, taking her by the arm to the retired nuns next door, for coffee and breakfast.

Romans can be profoundly selfish. You have to look very old indeed for anyone to give up their seat on a crowded tram, and they frequently fail to live up to all Christian virtues, and yet they have little time for inhumanity. Romans, like anyone else, get thoroughly fed up with their relatives and will complain about them freely, but they know they must look after them, as nothing else is acceptable. In Britain and the United States, as the coronavirus first began to strike, debates in the media and by politicians were as much about the economy as they were about possible fatalities. In Italy, of course people have been worried sick about their jobs and how they'll pay their bills, but the priority was always to save lives.

Saturday the 18th of April

Politics, populism and wickedness from the distant past

Plagues don't stop history. The epidemic that struck Athens in AD 430 did not stop the Peloponnesian War, any more than the Black Death brought the Hundred Years' War to a halt, or the Spanish Flu ended conflict in the trenches in France. So what of the never-ending conflict of Italian politics? What effect has coronavirus had here?

I should start by telling you a little about how Italian politics works. For almost half a century after the Second World War, the political situation was deceptive. To outsiders it seemed chaotic, with its frequent collapses of government and elections, but in fact it was highly stable. Italy was ruled by an irremovable coalition of several parties, which regularly fell out over who had how much power – and would call elections in the hope of improving their bargaining position – but in the end would always make a deal among themselves. This was the era of the Cold War and, with the approval of the United States, one of the largest parties, the Communist Party, was almost wholly excluded from national government.

This system came to an abrupt halt at the start of the 1990s when, with the end of the Cold War, Italy's ruling parties imploded in a series of corruption scandals. Ever since then, Italians have regarded their political parties rather as banks here regard their staff. At the bank I have an account with here, no sooner have I learned the name of one of the staff, and become able to make small talk with them, than they disappear. This, so I understand, is standard policy. After they have worked for a few years in one bank branch, staff are routinely moved on, for fear that they will become too knowledgeable about their customers' business affairs and may defraud them, or their customers will draw them into something illegal, such as tax avoidance.

In the early 1990s the Italians threw out their old, discredited parties and voted for new ones. One was the former Communist Party, now reinvented as the centre-left Partito Democratico or PD. Another was the Lega Nord party, which played on northern Italians' prejudice against southern Italian immigrants and campaigned for an independent state in the north, to be named Padania. A third new party was Silvio Berlusconi's Forza Italia (from a football chant, and meaning 'Come on Italy!'). In many ways Forza Italia was a trailblazer. Like Donald Trump, Berlusconi was a hugely wealthy individual who used new technology (his own empire of private TV channels) to appeal directly to voters, and who wasn't much troubled about his public image, or the veracity of his claims, so long as he hogged the limelight while his rivals languished in the shadows. So Italy has twice been a cauldron for the brewing of dubious political innovation: first Fascism and now modern populism.

In recent years, Italian voters have changed their allegiance yet again, and two new political parties have emerged. One is the Five Star Movement, the M5S, which was inspired by the grey-bearded stand-up comedian Beppe Grillo. This is a curious federation of special interest groups, from enthusiasts of direct democracy, to anti-vaxxers, to those who claim Wi-Fi is dangerous to people's health, so that it is hard to tell if the party is leftist or rightist, though its followers are passionately united against political corruption. The second new arrival was the Lega party. Under the leadership of Matteo Salvini this rose, phoenix-like, from the old Lega Nord – which had slumped following a corruption scandal – and was reinvented as a nationalist populist movement that redirected its fire from southern Italians to foreign immigrants.

Of course, nationalist populism is now a worldwide phenomenon. Across the globe movements have appeared which, like the Lega party, extensively employ social media to reach voters, attack political opponents without restraint, and show no squeamishness when it comes to a little mendacity, or scapegoating outsiders, notably immigrants. A number of these have flirted with autocratic rule and some have done more than flirt. Tayyip Erdoğan's regime in Turkey is close to being a dictatorship, as is Vladimir Putin's rule of Russia and, to the scandal of the EU, Viktor Orbán in Hungary is not far behind. With the help of the coronavirus crisis, Orbán has just added to his powers. Are we witnessing the beginning of the end of Western-style representative democracy? Will free speech soon be something to look back on with nostalgia? As it happens, Rome has twice witnessed the collapse of a fully functioning democratic system, and a quick glance at these transitional moments could offer up some clues as to our likely fate.

The first democratic collapse occurred more than two thousand years ago, with the fall of the Roman Republic. By modern standards this was barely recognizable as a democracy – it was clannish, dominated by aristocrats, and during the elections of officials, corruption was common – and yet there was genuine free speech, while the votes of the poorer plebeians could make a real difference in the choice of leaders. The plebeians also stood up for themselves. Well organized, they fought hard for their rights, both political and economic, and employed a radical form of strike action, marching out of the city en masse and decamping to a hill outside.

As to what brought the Roman Republic down, in part it was a victim of its own success: as its territory grew into an empire, it became increasingly hard to keep control of distant armies. But the Roman Republic was also killed by inequality. In its later years Rome became a slave economy. Rich Romans, keen to outdo one another in wealth, kicked poor farmers off their land so they could create large and highly profitable slave estates. Poor Romans in the city could not compete for employment with unpaid slaves and became dependent on state handouts. Over the centuries, vast wealth became concentrated in the hands of an ever-smaller number of people. Ordinary Romans, who had been at the heart of the old Republic, lost their sense of self-worth and ceased to feel a part of the system. Sounds familiar? It should do. With its citizen core eaten away, the Republic slowly succumbed to the ambitions of wannabe autocrats.

The second collapse of a democratic system here took place a century ago, when Italy's parliamentary constitutional monarchy fell to Fascism. Once again, the old system was far from perfect. It was dominated by wealthy families, too many Italians had no vote and there was corruption and clannishness. Yet it worked well enough. Voters felt their power and flung out governments they had ceased to support. There were radical changes of leadership between conservatives and socialists and a good number of people from modest backgrounds made their way to the top.

As to what killed it, it died of two maladies: war and fear. During the First World War Italians fought courageously, had a good number of successes and were on the winning side, but the cost was enormous. More than half a million

Italians died, many more were left disabled and when peace came the country was filled with angry, war-brutalized soldiers who felt their sacrifice had gone unrewarded. Mussolini sensed their resentment and channelled it to serve his own ends. All the while, many Italians – especially the wealthy, the conservative, and the religiously devout – were happy to give Fascism power because of their fear of something scarily alien: Russian Bolshevism.

I would say that these two examples from the past are both relevant to our own time. Many people in the West are turning their backs on established democratic parties because they have little self-worth. They're trapped in poverty in an increasingly unequal society that they don't feel fully part of. And they're frightened by the thought of a huge influx into their countries of something scarily alien and which they fear will further diminish their lives: immigrants. For democracies to work, they need citizens who feel they have a full stake in society.

For the moment I would say that the situation is still far from hopeless. Democracy should be flexible enough to represent new discontents and to answer them, rather than being broken by them. Italian politics looks less alarming than it did a few months ago and its saviour, rather surprisingly, has been the coronavirus. In summer 2019 Matteo Salvini left government to try to force elections he was confident he would win outright, only to find himself out-manoeuvred. The PD and M5S, formerly sworn enemies, made a deal and formed a government against him. It was an unstable coalition and by New Year it was fraying badly, but the parties have stuck together through the coronavirus crisis and are widely seen as having responded to it well. They've acted toughly and – once they realized the extent of the crisis – quickly, and more effectively than many other Western governments. Prime Minister Conte, who had no party political affiliation, has been much derided in the past. When the MS5 and the Lega formed a government in 2018, he was widely disparaged as a man who was only given the top job because neither of the coalition leaders would give it to the other. Yet he has emerged from the current situation as a statesman and Italy's most impressive leader for some time.

By contrast, Salvini, out of government, has been trying to tweet his way into the news with increasing desperation as the Covid crisis has escalated. At first he demanded that Italy should erect a frontier of steel to keep African migrants out, despite the fact that the epidemic wasn't in the south, where immigrants landed, but in the north. Next, he demanded that Italy should stay open for business, and that foreign tourists should continue to visit, denouncing claims that the health system was struggling with an epidemic as malicious fabrications. As the numbers of the dying swelled he abruptly changed tack and said the new lockdown should be even tougher, and that all transport and factories should be closed down. Later he changed again, saying that Italy's churches should open for Easter, as faith in science was not enough and God was needed too. All the while he used the crisis to attack the EU and Chinese immigrants. Though he undermined his own credibility when he was caught breaking the lockdown, walking by the Colosseum with his girlfriend.

Of course, these are early days. The economic slump that the coronavirus has brought about may play further into the hands of enemies of democracy. Once this eases the unstable coalition in Italy could collapse and Salvini may yet triumph at the polls. Yet I have some hope. It will be hard for populists in power to point the finger of blame elsewhere. Donald Trump may find the crisis strikes at his Achilles' heel – administrative competence – and if he goes, the seemingly unstoppable momentum of his copycats will weaken.

As with so much else these days, we'll just have to wait and see.

Rome's worst plague of all

The weather has turned rainy and mild. On my walk around our bubble just now I felt I could smell the scent of every leaf I passed. I might have been strolling in the country and the air, if it wasn't quite like champagne, was certainly a decent prosecco.

The news is good, too. Yesterday, I read the government's predictions of when the regions of Italy are expected to be free of new infections. Lombardy and Marche were listed last, and are not predicted to be contagion free till the end of June. Veneto and Piemonte, which have also been badly struck, came in at the end of May. As for our region of Lazio, it is estimated that we'll be free of new cases by mid-May, or in just over three weeks from now. Umbria is listed as post-contagion today! Of course, all of these calculations are based on data from a full lockdown, and improvement is likely to slow when this is eased.

Still, it's very encouraging, and it gives me enough optimism to face looking back to another plague which has afflicted Rome – its very worst. This was a disease that was dreaded in the city throughout its long history, and which took the lives of more Romans than any other. It had such a presence here that it shaped the very layout of Rome. It's not, as you may be thinking, Bubonic Plague – the Black Death. It's a disease we now associate with tropical countries, rather than Italy: malaria.

Malaria has probably been present in Rome since its earliest days and almost certainly helped decide the city's location on the seven hills (which were actually more like seven ridges). Italians are famous for their hilltop towns, and though hills were chosen partly for defence, there was another reason, too. Malarial mosquitoes are bad fliers and struggle to rise far above their watery hatching places. Though the early Italians didn't know that mosquitoes were the cause of the fevers that afflicted them, they knew that swampy lowlands were unhealthy. The Romans' first great project in the mid-seventh century BC, which marked their city's evolution from hilltop villages to an organized, Greek-style metropolis, was the draining of a swampy area between the hills to create the Forum, and it was probably done as much for reasons of health as to create a new city centre. Though it wasn't wholly successful, and from classical times right through to the nineteenth century, it was never wise to linger in the Forum after dark.

By the first century AD we have clear indications as to what kinds of malaria the Romans were suffering from. Among other sources, evidence comes from the same satirical poet, Juvenal, who was so venomous towards Greeks and easterners. His fourth satire is one of his finest, in which he attacks the sycophancy of Emperor Domitian's courtiers, who become poleaxed with fear when they are presented with a fish so huge that it is fit only for an emperor. In an aside, Juvenal mentions the season, 'when deadly autumn is giving way to winter frosts, and the sick dream of quartan fever'. Quartan fever was a mild form of malaria whose symptoms only became detectable when two other, nastier forms of the disease had passed. Romans at this time were suffering from three varieties of malaria at once.

Though not everyone was equally in peril. Those most at risk were children and new arrivals to the city, especially those from the north, who had no immunity. The poor were in much more danger than the rich. This was partly a matter of food – malnourishment made the disease more dangerous – and partly a matter of geography. Imperial Rome, which was the largest city on earth, had gradually extended from the original seven hills down into the low-lands by the Tiber. It was here, in today's Campo Marzio area, Testaccio and Trastevere, where malaria was prevalent, that the poor dwelt, while the rich still lived on the hills, which were healthier. Added to this was the fact that the rich could afford to escape Rome during the malarial season, from July to October, while the poor stayed and grew sick.

Throughout the coming centuries, malaria was a constant feature of Roman life. Among high-profile victims was

Alaric the Visigoth who, in AD 410, was the first man to sack Rome in eight hundred years. He died soon afterwards in Cosenza, Calabria, of a fever, which was almost certainly malaria he had contracted in Rome. He had been unwise to ravage the city in August, at the height of the malaria season.

Thanks to diseases, and especially to malaria, Rome was a demographic sinkhole, whose population was only maintained with the help of a constant flow of hungry and ambitious immigrants from the Italian countryside and abroad. Many will have expired soon after their arrival, from malaria. Yet the disease was also Rome's secret weapon. Romans had some immunity while foreigners, and especially northerners, did not. Pilgrims tried to time their trek south to avoid both Alpine snows and Roman fever. Malaria made Rome a hard place to capture. Attila the Hun's failure to march on Rome in AD 452 was probably because he feared malaria. Besieging armies had a short window in which to seize the city. Their best hope lay in bribing someone to open the gates – which happened repeatedly.

Some malarial seasons were worse than others. Every few years, Rome suffered a full epidemic which wreaked havoc on the city. These usually came after a period of late summer thunderstorms which turned low-lying areas of the city into waterlogged mosquito hatcheries. The consequences could be dramatic. In early August 1623, high churchmen gathered in the Vatican palace to choose a new pope. Within a short time, no fewer than eight cardinals and thirty of their high officials were dead. One could say they were victims of their own religion. The belief that Saint Peter's body had been buried in a cemetery in the low-lying area beneath the Vatican hill (which, as we have seen, may well be false) had been an important reason for the city's gradual slide from the hills to the malarial riverside. After the 1623 disaster, the popes relocated themselves and built an immense new palace on the Quirinal Hill, where they enjoyed two relatively malaria-free centuries.

All the while, medically minded Romans wondered how they were being infected with the disease. Though a few proposed that it was carried by mosquitoes, the idea was always dismissed on the grounds that there were areas of Italy that were rife with mosquitoes yet had no malaria (it wasn't yet understood that mosquitoes come in many varieties, and that of these only a few carry the disease). So it was ascribed to bad air – the *mal aria* that gives the disease its name.

Such thinking produced a small mystery during the nineteenth century. This was the era when wealthy northern Europeans and Americans wintered in Rome, socializing with one another and seeing the sights. Visitors included many great writers of the day, from Charles Dickens and Henry James to Nathaniel Hawthorne and John Ruskin, and most of these would pay a visit to the Roman Ghetto, to shake their heads at the outdated papal cruelty of locking away the city's Jews – and perhaps sneer a little at the Jews while they were about it. Some remarked on how strange it was that a summer evening's walk through the elegant, sweet-smelling Villa Borghese park could prove fatal, while the overcrowded slums of the ghetto were malaria-free and quite safe. The answer, which would not be understood for some time yet, was that the Villa Borghese was full of irrigated gardens that were a perfect breeding ground for mosquitoes, which could then hide among the leaves of plants, waiting for their victims. By contrast, the ghetto was so crowded that there was no space for gardens of any kind.

Rome would be cured of malaria decades before anybody understood why, and all thanks to politics. In 1870 the popes fled back to the Vatican and Rome became the capital of a unified Kingdom of Italy. It also became a building site, as ministries and apartment blocks sprang up for the country's new rulers, causing parkland to vanish and malaria quietly to retreat. Then again, it is far from unknown, when it comes to disease, for the cure to anticipate understanding. In the mid-nineteenth century medical thinking had changed surprisingly little since classical times – doctors still thought in terms of humours, and there was no knowledge of infection by microorganisms – yet people were healthier and lived longer than they ever had before, all because their customs had changed. They bathed and washed their clothes more frequently than in earlier times.

The coronavirus is a useful reminder that our lives have changed rather less over the centuries than we might suppose. The responses to the epidemic, by governments and individuals, have been very similar to responses to disease outbreaks in other eras: an initial reluctance to accept what's happening, a false confidence that it will strike others and not oneself, excitement and hedonism as the disease comes closer, and then fear and irrationality when it fully breaks out, along with an eagerness to find somebody to blame. Of course, we're far better off than our ancestors in all kinds of ways. We have sophisticated hospitals whose staff are skilled at keeping people alive; we're cleaner, as it's far easier to wash our hands and our clothes than it was in the past; we're well organized and good at disseminating information on how to deal with a disease; we're very quick to know about a new epidemic, and to respond to it – which is just as well, as we're also much quicker to spread it all around the globe.

And yet our best defence today is precisely what it always was. Safety lies in avoiding others, isolating ourselves and waiting till the worst danger has passed. It's an approach that has not changed since Boccaccio's time in the 1340s, when, in his *Decameron*, his characters flee to a villa outside Florence and tell one another stories as the Black Death rages. As a strategy, it's so simple that it has proved a great leveller. Relatively poor lands, such as Sri Lanka or the Indian province of Kerala, appear to be doing well against coronavirus, while countries that are wealthy and organized – including the UK and the USA – have made a real dog's dinner of the crisis. Poorer countries may even have a slight advantage, in that they have not forgotten how dangerous epidemics can be, while the West has enjoyed the illusion that such worries are a thing of the past.

Interior decorating and paganism

The one thing that has most worried me since this lockdown began – aside, of course, from getting the coronavirus – is our flat. In these days, when we're at home almost all the time, the last thing we want is for a vital device to go wrong, and now something has. A bathroom pump, which caused flooding in the past, warping floorboards in another room, has begun making an ominous, strained noise and we've stopped using the bathroom. I rather doubted we'd be able to find anyone to deal with it, as such a thing hardly seems essential, but we were lucky and a repair man came this morning, suitably masked and gloved. He kept his distance, as did we, and the pump now works.

Buying property in Rome can be a tricky process. In the UK you need a surveyor to check the building is structurally sound, but in Italy people rather assume that it won't fall down and the one professional person they'll always hire is a lawyer, to make sure there's no fraudulent surprise lurking. Does the seller actually own the place they're selling? Is the property linked to a mountain of unpaid utility bills or taxes? Or, the most common trouble of all, have changes been made to the property that weren't correctly registered with the authorities, and so are illegal? If your lawyer hasn't done a good job, your property may have irregularities that you'll only discover years later when you try to sell. Sometimes people have to bring in builders to change everything back to how it was, twenty or even fifty years before. This is especially annoying if the illegal changes were an improvement that greatly added to the property's appeal.

Our experience of finding a flat was made more complicated by our need, first of all, to pick a country. We'd been in Rome for a few years and the time had arrived when we wondered if we were being self-indulgent to live in this beautiful, impractical city, and should move to a more sober place. It's a moment that comes to many foreigners living here. Some leave and have no regrets. Others sell their car at a knockdown price, give up the flat that they fought so hard to get – and which has such a beautiful view – and go, only to return a year or so later, and begin struggling to set up their life all over again. Rome can do that. It has a way of pulling you back. It's not that it's perfect, or even adequate, but if its good qualities appeal to you, it has a way of ruining everywhere else.

Fortunately, we only looked into leaving. We spent a few weeks in the UK, interrogating friends there about their lives – what did they find annoying? What did they like and hate? – and being alarmed by the expense of property.

Then we did the same thing in Vancouver. At the end of it all, we decided we might as well stay where we were, but stop haemorrhaging money on rent and buy somewhere. I began touring Rome, looking at flats, happily ignorant of the fact that I was in a bubble that was about to burst. We just managed to put down money on a flat and take on a mortgage before the 2007 banking crisis began.

For all that, I'm glad we did what we did. A home, even bought at a bad price, is still a home and we're lucky to own one. Besides, the price wasn't too crazy, thanks to Oliver, the estate agent we bought the property through. Oliver's outlook on life, I should explain, was a curious mixture of practicality and dreamer. He grew up in East Germany and in November 1989 the dreamer in him took charge. When others were breaking off sections of the Berlin Wall as souvenirs, he stepped round them and made his way directly to Rome, which he knew little about except that it was where he wanted to be. Here, his practical side kicked in and, seeing how dismal the employment options were for foreigners, he went for one of the few professions that could offer a decent income, and he became an estate agent.

His practicality showed itself again with the sellers of our flat. It was co-owned by no fewer than six siblings, five men and a woman, whose grandfather had bought the flat soon after the building was first constructed, and all of whom were now thoroughly grown up. Concerned that a sale might be delayed interminably by disagreements among the six,

Oliver insisted that he should set the price and that there could be no negotiation. In return he'd charge the family no commission. The figure he chose was correct for the property at that time and, having looked at dozens of flats, almost all of them far from desirable, and on offer at prices that were wildly optimistic, I knew, even before I'd stepped inside the place, that we had to go for it. And so we did.

I'd recommend Oliver to anyone thinking of buying a flat in Rome, except that he no longer works in the business. His dreamer side took charge once again. When he first showed us round the flat he told us that he had a great passion for dogs – he had a Labrador – and that the high point of his year was going to the Crufts dog show in London. He has now set up a dog-training centre in the south-west of Rome. The logo, suitably enough, is modelled on the famous Michelangelo image from the Sistine Chapel, of God's outstretched finger as he creates Adam, though in this case the finger reaches out to a paw. If I ever find myself with an unruly dog, that's where I'll go.

If we were lucky with Oliver, we were also lucky with our builders. These were two brothers, Massimo and Pietro, who came strongly recommended by Roman friends of ours whose judgement I trusted. Massimo and Pietro had a major job to do. The apartment had hardly been touched for decades and was a strange place, chopped into numerous, poky rooms to house the family of eight who'd lived there, and filled with wooden figures of the Virgin Mary.

Almost all the partition walls had to go. Unfortunately, Rome's city authority – the *Comune* – was remaking the pavement below the building, which meant Massimo and Pietro could not get permission to set up a rubble chute from the windows, while the building's condominium assembly forbade them to use the lift. The two of them bought heavy-duty backpacks and proceeded to carry the rubble downstairs, day after day, and to heave sections of partition up. They never complained once.

They worked quickly, finished the job not just on time but earlier than promised, and didn't go one euro over budget. And they did an excellent job. If you happen to need a flat redone in Rome, I'd strongly recommend them. Of the various problems we've had over the years, none stemmed from their work and all resulted from aesthetic concern. But I should explain. Everybody wants their home to look good, of course, but you also want it to function. In Rome, though, appearance comes first. In shops, searching for the right sink or tap or bathroom tile – a task that seemed never to end – if I raised practicalities (Was this well made? Would it last?) I'd feel like a blasphemer in church and I'd be told, '*Ma signore, è più bello*' (It's more beautiful). In consequence we have, among other things, a fridge whose doors are bizarrely hard to close and which frequently breaks down (my greatest concern during this lockdown) and a bathroom pump that, as you've seen, causes occasional destruction.

At the risk of another dose of national stereotyping, I would say that aesthetics is a big part of most Romans' outlook, and not only when it comes to their homes. In the UK to look a little scruffy is seen as good manners and to be too well-dressed smacks of showing off. In Rome you're expected to look reasonably smart (fortunately for me, exceptions are made for foreigners). Romans pay attention to the appearance of everything, from buildings to shop windows to the food on your plate in a restaurant. People here have a good visual sense and the appearance of things is part of Rome's charm. And yet, when I stop to think of it, all of this does seem a little strange in the city that is the headquarters of the world's leading Christian Church. When Christianity first began to grow into a major religion, it preached simplicity, modesty, poverty and humility. Martyrdom and virginity were ideals. Early Christians were urged to spurn excessive wealth, over-flavoursome and spicy food, showy clothes and, most of all, sexiness. Even sex within marriage was considered a little shabby, while extra-marital sex of any kind was regarded as wickedly sinful, as was flirting or showing off one's body. Plain was best.

There's little sign of this thinking today. A common summer sight here is young Roman couples on motorbikes heading for the beach to work on their perfect tan, barely clothed apart from their helmets (I dread to think what happens to them if they have an accident and hit the tarmac). Likewise, Roman food, I'm very happy to say, is anything but plain. Nor do the Romans shy away from wealth, if it's there to be had. All in all, Saint Paul would have been horrified by the antics of Silvio Berlusconi, yet that didn't stop him winning elections. Rome may be the world's leading Christian capital, yet in some ways the Romans seem distinctly pagan.

Are Romans really such bad drivers?

With relaxation of the lockdown only ten days away, the Italian government is turning its thoughts to what should be done about transport? How can social distancing be maintained on Rome's buses and trams? It will be no easy matter, seeing as they're frequently packed like sardine cans.

The authorities have been paying close attention to Wuhan, where the lockdown ended a couple of weeks ago, and where many people, who still feel understandably anxious, have avoided public transport, preferring to drive. If Romans do the same, as is likely, we can expect crammed roads. The government is considering setting up a network of new cycle lanes, which would be a very welcome change, especially as Rome has made shamefully few concessions to cyclists till now. There's a proposal to use the road around the city walls, which would include our street, and to employ people to make sure drivers stick to the rules. I'd welcome all of these ideas, though I'll believe them when I see them.

At the moment the main change the virus has brought to Rome's roads – aside from emptying them – is that some Romans now drive as if they're on quiet, country lanes, hurtling about so fast that as a pedestrian you really have to keep a look out. It's just the sort of behaviour that confirms Romans' reputation for terrible driving. But is this justified?

It's not easy to get an Italian driving licence. We know this because Shannon had to get one, for reasons that are complex, not very interesting and which I'll explain as briefly as I can. In Canada driving licences are issued by provinces, which means there is no national licence and which further means there can't be a reciprocal arrangement allowing Canadians to exchange their licence for an Italian one (this is true for the USA, too, but almost nowhere else). Shannon went to our local office of ACI, the Automobile Club d'Italia, which is the Italian equivalent of the AA, and handles everything to do with driving, from paying car tax to renewing one's licence, to learning to drive. She signed up for a course and joined a class filled with teenagers and middle-aged nuns – two especially hazardous types of Roman driver.

The test itself was easy. Driving around quiet streets in Monteverde, just above our home, Shannon's only problem was the examiner, who was so excited to have a Canadian candidate that she distracted her with endless questions, causing Shannon to make at least one heinous infraction of the rules. Shannon was quite convinced she'd failed, but the examiner had either been too busy talking to notice, or had felt forgiving, and had decided that a North American forty-something would be safe enough on Rome's roads.

The most difficult part was the written exam. This was taken on computers in a large shed-like building on the other side of Rome and was multiple choice. Shannon had studied hard for weeks as she'd seen how tricky the questions could be. Some seemed contrived to catch you out, tempting you with a choice that all common sense suggested was correct, but was worded in such a way as to be wrong. Again, Shannon's North American respectability proved an asset. As she was puzzling over one especially fiendish choice, a stern-looking invigilator came up to her, pointed at the screen and murmured, 'Well I wouldn't choose those. Nor that one.' Only one possibility remained.

Considering how hard it is to get a licence, you'd think that Romans would drive very carefully, but no. Their worst habit is to dart out in front of you from a side road, so you have to brake sharply – something that happens frequently. Worse still are the motorcyclists, who swerve out from nowhere, terrifying in their vulnerability. It's all too common to see one who has been knocked off his bike, lying stretched out on the tarmac, with a garment folded up beneath their head, like a pillow, and guarded by whoever was riding pillion. Happily, this is usually precautionary – for fear of neck injuries – and after a time they get to their feet, none too worse for wear. Of course, some never get up, and there are private shrines around the city to commemorate them.

Rome's motorways require particular care, especially to anyone unused to them. Whether from lack of space or to save costs, some sections have alarmingly sharp turns for a motorway, and troubling junctions where drivers exit and join in the same short stretch of road. Connections with popular out-of-town shopping areas can be bewilderingly maze-like, and even after numerous visits to one outside Rome, I still get lost. But worst of all is the city centre late at night. Either drivers at this hour are younger, or the darkness makes them more reckless, but there's no doubt that they're wilder behind the wheel. If possible I try to avoid driving in Rome at this time.

And yet I wouldn't say Romans are poor drivers. They're both skilful and dangerous. In more northerly countries, where roads are better designed, drivers may get into trouble through lack of concentration. In remote areas of Australia and Canada they sometimes succumb from sheer boredom. Roman drivers, by contrast, are fearsomely alert. Though most are sensible enough, a large minority regards driving as a sport. They go too fast and take needless risks in over-taking, which is rarely a necessity – Romans are rarely in a hurry – but is seen as an end in itself. In a genuine emergency there's a clear protocol. The driver blasts on the horn while a passenger holds a piece of cloth – anything will do – out of the window. Other drivers understand and allow the car to pass.

August is the best season to drive in Rome. It's not only that the roads are quiet, but also the lack of other drivers to compete with has a soothing effect on those who remain, who drive much more sedately than in other seasons. If you've really had enough of Roman drivers then you can always head north. Once you leave Rome's ring road, the GRA, behind you and reach country towns you'll be amazed at how friendly and considerate everyone is on the road. Reach Tuscany or Umbria and you'll find the roads themselves are noticeably improved – better designed and maintained, with fewer potholes and kamikaze junctions. Finally, if you want to think better of Roman drivers, just go south. Spend a few days in Naples and when you get back, you'll feel like you're driving through Switzerland.

How to survive Roman red tape, and what it taught me about Brexit

With police stopping people across Italy, it's no surprise that a number of cases of bizarre rule-breaking have reached the attention of the newspapers. Some involve pitifully bad liars. A man in Vibo Valentia, in the southern region of Calabria, claimed he'd gone out to have lunch in the hospital cafeteria, only to change his story when the police pointed out that the hospital had no cafeteria. Others are simply shameless. A couple were stopped on their way to the supermarket in Lucca, Tuscany. When the police said only one family member was permitted to go out shopping, the wife yelled at them, 'But I can't let my husband go by himself. He always buys the wrong things.'

Other cases are just sad. A seventeen-year-old girl in Forlì in Emilia-Romagna broke the rules, left her home and was arrested beneath the apartment of her ex-boyfriend. He'd called the police to be rid of her. A teenager from Albano, just outside Rome, had ticked the box on his self-declaration form to say he was going out for *reasons of urgent necessity*. When stopped by the police, he said that he needed to feed the pigeons. He then added that he was homeless, as his mother and grandmother didn't want him around anymore.

Finally, there are the overly honest. A 33-year-old, who was found wandering near the Franchi stadium in Florence, had written on his auto-certification form that he was going out to find a dealer and buy drugs. The police, rather generously, allowed him to revise his motive.

We are now on our third self-declaration form, the authorities having changed the wording twice early on in the lockdown, as the rules were tightened. It looks like we'll soon be filling in a fourth version as, when the lockdown is eased, there'll still be rules and restrictions and we'll still need to carry the document. Overall, I see them as a fairly sensible measure. There's nothing like completing a long and tiresome form to make you question if you really need to go out. But they're also a very Italian approach to the crisis. This is a land where paperwork is king.

For anyone who comes here from the UK, Roman red tape can seem both tiresome and a little absurd. When we first arrived, and thought we were on an adventure for only a year or so, I did the minimum required. Shannon and I each got our permission-to-stay documents – the *permesso di soggiorno* – and then our social security numbers but we went no further. On a bus, when I happened to see an expat proudly showing another expat his Italian residence card, I felt scornful of such slavish obedience to paperwork. I would have none of it.

But of course I did. When we decided to buy a flat it made sense to take up Italian residency, to pay Italian taxes and to take a mortgage with an Italian bank. I became very familiar with Roman bureaucratic offices as I got us our health cards and identity cards. I felt quite a sense of triumph when I managed to execute a highly complex manoeuvre and changed from being a British Roman resident to a German Roman resident (a useful thing to do in Brexit times).

In the unlikely event that anyone reading this account ever finds themselves in a Roman bureaucratic office, I'll now pass on what wisdom I've learned over the years. Most of all, never get angry, however annoying and illogical the situation in which you find yourself, and however rude and obdurate the person you're dealing with. Lose your temper and any hope you have of securing the golden wonder you're seeking – a piece of paper with a stamp and signature on it – will be gone. Stay polite, look a little sad and you're still in the game. Your adversary may begin to feel sorry for you. Or, more likely, they'll tire of you. Because here's another piece of advice. Once you have a seat opposite a government official – and it can take weeks to get one – don't give that seat up. If they tell you three times that there's absolutely nothing that can be done, just stay in your seat, looking confused and sorrowful. It's astonishing how often this approach yields results. Reluctantly the official will find a solution – just to get you out of the room.

Try and feel some compassion for the official you're dealing with. Remember, they probably don't want to be in this office any more than you do. They have a safe job, certainly, but it's not exciting. As a foreigner you have an advantage over Romans who are in your position: you're a welcome distraction in a dull day. If the civil servant you're dealing with wants to lighten their morning with a discussion of UK football teams, or UK politics, or fond memories of a teenage school trip to London, oblige them. It's the very least you can do.

Also, understand that the rules they're working within are often fiendishly complicated, and that this can put them in a difficult situation. On the one hand, they don't want to approve something that is not permitted and which could get them into trouble. On the other hand, they may not have a clear idea of what *is* permissible. That's why they get angry and tell you nothing can be done – they're anxious. Most bureaucratic employees are nervous of dealing with anything that isn't routine. But in some back room there will almost always be somebody who understands all the rules, however complex, and knows exactly what's what. Hence the need to stay in your seat. If you prove irritating enough, the person you're dealing with may take you to the resident expert and then, as if by magic, everything will be resolved.

Timing can also be useful. I once chose to attempt what I knew was an absurdly over-ambitious procedure. I wanted to have Alexander and Tatiana's residency changed from

British to German and to get them permanent Italian residency all at once. I was certain I'd bitten off more than I could chew. By chance, the only appointment that worked for us all was one morning between Christmas and New Year. I'll long remember that day as it was little less than miraculous. I'd never dreamed I might see documents inspected, interviews concluded and papers printed out, stamped and signed so rapidly. I know why. I'd noticed that everyone in the office had an aura of excited anticipation. They had a big Christmas lunch planned.

Finally, don't forget that you're in Rome, and that if you dig a little, there's a good chance that you'll strike a vein of humanity. There are a number of times when I have found myself in a government office and an official has given me a faint, confiding smile, to tell me they find some rule just as idiotic as I do. One day when Shannon was in the midst of preparing for her Italian driving exam, a stony-faced ACI official told her that she had missed her chance to take it in English, as the option was about to be abolished and the last English exam slots were already filled. Shannon burst into tears. Miraculously, a way for her to take the exam in English was found. Our Italian friends afterwards praised her response and told her that she couldn't have handled the situation better.

In our early days here, in another overreaching moment, I went to an office in the hope of getting a social security number, not only for myself – which would have been straightforward – but also for Shannon and for Alexander, who was only a few months old, though neither of them could come with me. After being directed from one official to another, I was finally sent to a senior figure who gave me a hard look and asked, 'Your wife, why isn't she here?' I told her, 'She's at home with the baby.' I'd only said it because it was true, but I saw her eyes soften. I had all our social security numbers within moments.

After years of dealing with Italian bureaucracy I realize something strange has happened. My English way of seeing things has quietly melted away. I now see that, tiresome though the Italian system can be, it's not always wrong. Being expected to carry an identity card doesn't seem like tyranny. For that matter it can be rather handy, if your car has been towed and you need to show that you're the owner, or if you are knocked over by a tram and the authorities need to alert your relatives. It's very useful if you want to apply for Italian citizenship and need to prove how long you've been living in the country. I know Italian officialdom isn't always welcoming towards poor immigrants, and I'm sure it isn't easy for them to find their way through the bureaucratic labyrinth, yet the paperwork required offers them some protection. I can't imagine a Windrush scandal happening here. People who have rightfully lived and worked and paid taxes here would never find themselves, fearful of forced deportation, desperately searching for decades-old gas bills to prove their presence in the country. They'll be on the system.

Getting to know Roman red tape has given me an understanding of something else, too – Brexit. At the risk of making myself unpopular with some readers, I feel I need to come clean here. Ever since Britain joined the Common Market in 1973, I've been keenly pro-European. I felt that European countries acting together would have a voice in the world that would be heard, and which would offer a useful counterbalance to America, Russia and China. I won't claim that the EU is perfect, yet I don't feel its failings are all its own doing. It grew into a bureaucratic institution because national governments weren't prepared to let it emerge as a truly legitimate rival to their power. Though it has been much criticized in recent years, its achievements are still impressive. It has helped countries, from Spain and Greece to Latvia, to evolve from economically backward former dictatorships to affluent democracies, and though some are struggling now, both in their wealth and their politics, they're far better off than they were before they joined.

Yet I have to say that, though I was profoundly saddened when Britain voted to leave the EU, thanks to my apprenticeship in Roman bureaucracy I wasn't wholly surprised. Roman red tape may be especially bad but one can find versions of it from Lisbon to Helsinki, and from Oslo to Athens. I'm afraid I'm descending into generalizations once again, yet I feel there's a truth here. While there is immense diversity across the continent of Europe, I would say that deep down all of its countries have something in common, which is at odds with the British approach. In Britain, at the centre of people's thinking – and many politicians' thinking – is the idea of individual liberty. On the continent the ideal is something different: good citizenship and social harmony. In my experience most British people strongly resent being told what to do, by the state or by each other, and more so than most Europeans. Most Europeans have a distaste for unruly citizens or social disharmony, more so than many Brits. Of course, these ideals aren't always realized. British people constantly find themselves told what to do, by the state and by each other, and have to put up with it, while continental Europeans have to endure social disharmony and misbehaviour by their fellow citizens. Yet the ideals, however battered they may be, remain in people's thoughts.

Across Europe, there's enthusiasm for the idea of an efficient system. In the UK the idea of systems is frequently met with suspicion, as something that smacks of foreignness and dictatorship. In Europe, all the other countries have a form of written political constitution, while in Britain politics is governed by reference to an accumulation of decisions from the past. European and British law have the same distinction. In Europe, it's often seen as no bad thing for the state to play a significant role in the economy and in people's lives. In Britain, such a thing is regarded much more warily, and many feel the state's powers need to be constantly watched and curbed. I'm probably going way too far here, but I wonder if it can even be applied in their approach to the arts, whether a French or a German novelist will start with a theme, while a British writer is more likely to begin with a situation and a character or two – of course both writers will probably end up in much the same place.

Finally, there's the English Channel and all that history. Looking through British – and especially English – eyes, the continent of Europe may be charming for holidays but it's also a large and dangerous place that intermittently spits out Viking raiders, Spanish Armadas, Napoleonic fleets, Zeppelins and Heinkels. It's a place of threat whose nations are better divided among themselves, so they'll pose less of a danger. From this side of the water things look very different. The continent of Europe is a family that, like it or not, you're a part of. It's a highly dysfunctional family, no denying it, whose members have inflicted all kinds of brutalities on one another over the centuries – along with kindnesses – but it's your family nevertheless.

Having grown up in Britain, it took me a while to understand that when Romans told me what to do – warning me to wrap up our baby more warmly on a cold day, or telling me to be careful walking down some steps – this wasn't aggressive or controlling, but was meant kindly, and was the performance of a civic duty. Now I'm quite used to it and offer my thanks, though I'm not so acculturated that I think of doing such a thing back. I understand both mentalities and can see good in both. Though I have to say that in this present crisis, identity cards and a little state bossiness have proved rather useful.

What makes me saddest is that I have no doubt that Britain's different approach made it particularly valuable in Europe. British practicality and pragmatism were a useful balance to continental idealism. For many years I've sensed that Britain's continuance within the EU was fragile, yet I hoped it might continue. Sadly, it's not to be.

Saturday the 25th of April

Liberation Day and Roman criminality

Today is Liberation Day. Seventy-five years ago, the National Committee for the Liberation of Upper Italy called on all northern Italians to rise up against the occupying German forces. Within days, Nazi forces in Italy had surrendered, Mussolini was dead and Italy's war was finally over.

Liberation Day is not among the biggest holidays here. National Day on the second of June, May Day and New Year all have a higher profile, as, of course, do Christmas and Easter, and yet in normal times a good number of events are held in Rome to mark the moment. Last year, Italy's president, Sergio Mattarella, placed a wreath on the tomb of the unknown soldier on the Vittoriano monument in Rome and members of the National Association of Italian Partisans gathered at the Ardeatine Caves – the site of a notorious Nazi massacre. There were also events by Jewish Romans and anti-Fascists, and a film about the occupation and liberation was projected onto the stone side of the ancient Pyramid of Cestius. This year, there are similar events taking place, but without any watching crowds. Liberation celebrations are being watched online.

Though to make things a little less dull, the *Frecce Tricolori* – the Italian Air Force's acrobatic team, and equivalent of the RAF's Red Arrows – flew over Rome. They passed right above our apartment, leaving a trail of red, white and green smoke, and soon afterwards I heard distant neighbours singing the Italian national anthem.

Liberation Day seems a little taunting right now, with everybody stuck in their homes. No doubt many will have struggled with the claustrophobia of the lockdown and, unhappily, in some cases it has brought out people's worst natures. A national association, Women on the Web Against Violence, which is based in Rome, has reported that the number of women seeking help has more than doubled during the lockdown. Likewise, the Italian press has reported a number of horrific cases of lockdown crime during recent weeks. Here in Rome, a nineteen-year-old, whose name has only been given as Valerio, murdered and decapitated his mother. A few days ago, in a suburb of Milan, a woman tram driver, Alessandra Città, was murdered by her former lover, a labourer from Trentino, Antonio Vena. Both originally came from Sicily and for some years they had been involved in a long-distance relationship, in which Vena would stay with Città at weekends. She ended the affair just before the lockdown in Lombardy was announced but, as Vena could not go home, she unwisely said he could stay on. After a quiet dinner he made advances to her and when she refused him, he fetched a rifle she kept in the home and shot her dead. Immediately afterwards he went to the police and confessed, 'I've killed my lover.' This was the third lockdown murder in Lombardy. In the other two, husbands killed their wives and then themselves.

Yet not all lockdown victims are women. A month ago in Turin, Emanuele Trimboli rang his sister and told her their father was dead. When she hurried to the flat where her father and brother lived, she found her father lying stabbed to death in the kitchen. Her brother was arrested soon afterwards. The strangest and saddest lockdown murder was in Genoa, where a woman, Giulia Stanganini, took a taxi to the police station and told them that her mother had hanged herself several days earlier and that she had cut the body into pieces. The police were initially disbelieving, but when they visited Stanganini's flat they duly found her mother's body in several buckets and plastic bags. Neighbours reported that Giulia had moved in with her mother some weeks before and that they were always arguing. Investigations revealed that Giulia had endured a string of misfortunes. Her marriage had ended, she had been unemployed for some while and the previous November her three-year-old son had become ill and had died in hospital. During extensive questioning Giulia adamantly kept to her story that her mother had hanged herself and that, the night before she went to the police, she had chopped up the body. Curiously, the police have not ruled out the possibility of someone outside the family being involved in the killing.

After the various murders and attempted murders I've described in this account, you may imagine Rome is a dangerous city. I'm happy to say that the opposite is true. Rome is in fact unusually safe for a capital city of three million people. Despite all the efforts of organized crime, Italy has the lowest murder rate among European states – leaving out the tiny ones like Andorra – and one of the lowest in the world. The homicide rate in the UK is almost twice as high, in the USA it is nearly tenfold higher, and in El Salvador (currently the world's worst place for murder) you are a hundred times more likely to be killed than you are in Italy. Nor is Rome dangerous by Italian standards. Milan is the country's homicide capital, as well as being bad for sexual violence, infanticide and armed robbery, Naples is top for muggings and theft, and Trieste is the country's fraud centre. By contrast, Rome is low on the list for violent crimes and highest for drug dealing and production.

The one criminal activity that I take care to warn all visitors about is pickpocketing, which is a real problem. I don't want to exaggerate the danger, and in eighteen years I've yet to be robbed, but it's a good idea to be careful. If you're out seeing the sights, you're well advised to leave your passport where you're staying and to keep your wallet and phone carefully zipped away, and preferably zipped twice over, in a compartment of a backpack or bag. If you feel you're in a dodgy spot, carry your backpack on your front, where nobody can open it unobserved. Women are wise to keep handbags tight beneath their arms and with the strap, if it's long enough, round their necks.

Certain places are especially bad. These include all the main tourist areas, such as the Colosseum, the Forum area and St Peter's. You need to take care in the Campo de' Fiori market when it's crowded in high season, and our huge local Sunday flea market, Porta Portese, where people are wedged tightly between the stalls, is also bad, as are the trams and buses that bring people there. For half a century and more the 64 bus, which runs from Termini to the Vatican, has been famous for pickpockets. Rome's two metro lines are also risky, especially beneath Termini station, which has plenty of tunnels for a thief to flee down.

Romans are by no means immune to having their pockets picked, though unaware tourists make the easiest targets. As to the pickpockets, these are often easier to spot than one might think. Some double as beggars – if their begging distracts and offers a chance of theft, so much the better. On buses and trams a common ploy is for a group of male pickpockets to stand by the doors pretending to be drunk and then get in everybody's way when passengers try to get off, which allows for pushing and confusion as passengers, worried they'll miss their stop, try to get past them. Having got what they want, the thieves then move down the tram or bus as quickly as they can, exit through the next set of doors and flee.

The same manoeuvre is also done in reverse. Years ago, Shannon and I found ourselves sitting with a very young Alexander on the infamous 64 bus, which was waiting to start up and was still almost empty. Next to us sat a group of young women with babies, and we got talking to them, comparing notes on baby behaviour and baby care. Finally, the driver switched on the engine, more passengers began hurrying aboard, the four young women said their farewells and got up to push against the swell and, I have no doubt, to try and rob people. It was a strange moment. I'd liked them, though I wished they'd found a less cruel way to make a living. Though so far I've been lucky and have only suffered false alarms, mistakenly thinking my wallet's gone, I know that horrible feeling of panic, and of dread at the thought of all the bureaucratic offices I'd have to visit to replace my health card, driving licence and identity card. Then again, who knows what other options the women had?

Pickpocketing and drug dealing aren't the only criminal activities that take place in Rome. There are plenty of other goings-on that are far more wicked but are harder to unearth. The sins of the Vatican, financial and sexual, have been written about a great deal, but less well known, at least outside Italy, are the dubious dealings within Rome's civic administration. I mentioned in an earlier diary entry how, during an especially bad autumn thunderstorm, roads flooded and cars floated away. It was only some years after this happened that I learned that it was not only bad weather that had been to blame. In June 2013, Romans elected a new mayor, Ignazio Marino, who had previously had a glittering career as a transplant surgeon. Shortly after he took office, Marino was approached by members of a criminal syndicate who offered him money if he turned a blind eye to their activities. Marino contacted the judicial authorities and opened the Rome *Comune*'s books to the *Guardia di Finanza* – Italy's finance police. So began a scandal that the press dubbed *Mafia Capitale*.

One can forgive the Romans for having a weakness for conspiracy theories. When the first thirty-seven arrests were made, in early December 2014, they included the former head of Rome's rubbish collection service, AMA, the president of Rome's assembly, the assembly's transparency officer and the former chief of police for the region of Rome. Under investigation but not yet arrested was Marino's predecessor as mayor, Gianni Alemanno. At the heart of the scandal were figures who were anything but establishment. Chief among them was Massimo Carminati, a one-eyed neo-fascist and former member of a terrorist group, *Nuclei Armati Rivoluzionari*, which has been implicated in the infamous 1980 bombing of Bologna station, in which eighty people died. Carminati has also been accused of the murder, two years earlier, of two students in Milan, and was a member of Rome's infamous Magliana gang, which was at the centre of the city's organized crime in the 1970s and early 80s.

Carminati's chief accomplice in *Mafia Capitale* was Salvatore Buzzi, who won hugely lucrative contracts for managing welcome centres for refugees, for running the infamously badly maintained encampments of Romani people, and managing Rome's parks and green areas. In a telephone call that was taped by the police, Buzzi boasted, 'You have no idea how much I can make out of these immigrants. They pay far better than drugs.' Buzzi's companies were also responsible for clearing leaves from Rome's drains, and it was because this work had been neglected for years, and the drains had become blocked, that the thunderstorms in 2010 caused such chaos in the city. But whatever failings Buzzi had, one can't fault his honesty. At the end of 2012 he sent out a text message to welcome in the New Year: 'Let's hope that 2013 will be a year full of garbage, refugees, immigrants, homeless kids – a whole blizzard of them – as that's a new crop of grass to mow. Long live social cooperation!'

As to how much Roman taxpayers had been defrauded by the scandal, when the first arrests were made at the end of 2013, prosecutors confiscated over 200 million euros of property. From Carminati they seized more than fifty artworks, including some by Andy Warhol and Jackson Pollock.

In the end justice was done, at least to an extent. A number of figures were convicted, including Carminati and Buzzi, who were sentenced to twenty and nineteen years respectively, reduced slightly on appeal. Marino's predecessor as mayor, Gianni Alemanno, was given six years. Yet, rather than being hailed as a hero, Marino was persecuted by the many enemies he had made. When he first refused to take the gangsters' money he found himself the subject of a series of bizarre fake accusations, which became known as Pandagate, concerning supposed parking violations that involved his Fiat Panda. After the *Mafia Capitale* scandal broke, despite the fact that he had been notable for his modest spending – he refused to use a government car, preferring to cycle, and declined to employ a state-paid bodyguard – he was accused of fiddling expenses. After barely two years in office, Marino resigned in order to fight this last accusation, and though it was summarily dismissed by the courts, by then he had tired of politics and decided to go back to his work as a surgeon.

In a way one could regard this dreadful business as the flip side to Romans' talent for connecting with one another. As I've recounted, this is a city where personal relationships are key. That's the reason why, when you become a regular at a coffee bar, you'll find the smiling barista has made your particular choice of coffee before you've even had a chance to order. Pride is taken in remembering both you and the coffee you drink. But it's also the reason why, once you're a known customer at a bar or shop, you're no longer given a receipt. You may also get a small discount. You've been welcomed into a tiny conspiracy to defraud the government of a few centesimi of tax. It would take a very cold and correct individual to say no.

Of course, none of this is any excuse for the exploitation of the poor and vulnerable, or for stealing from taxpayers, or for abusing the trust given to an official of the government. When I first came to live in Rome I might have found the *Mafia Capitale* scandal amusing, but I've been here too long now to stand back and smile, or to point a holier-than-thou finger. This is my city now and this kind of corruption makes me feel ashamed. Being an honorary Roman comes at a price.

Is Roman cuisine really any good?

Last night the Italian prime minister, Conte, gave details
of how the lockdown will be eased in phase two, which
is to begin a week from today. One of Shannon's Italian
work colleagues described Conte, rather unkindly, as 'a
void wearing a mask', and a number of people have complained that his message was complicated and unclear. One
Internet comment was, 'You'll be permitted to leave your
home only if you can understand what Conte said.' I felt he
came across fairly well – concerned and serious. I'd much
rather have him in charge of my fate than Donald Trump.
Or, for that matter, Boris Johnson, who squandered six
weeks of precious time when he could have been preparing the NHS for the virus, and who was still talking about
herd immunity when Bergamo's health system was being
overwhelmed by sick and dying people.

The biggest change that Conte mentioned, of course, is
that we will have something like free movement. We'll be
able to travel freely anywhere within the region of Lazio. So
long as we all wear masks and maintain social distancing,
we can visit our relatives (except that we don't have any

here). Parks will be reopened. Social gatherings in people's homes will still be prohibited, and bars and restaurants won't open fully till the 1st of June (virus permitting) but restaurants will be allowed to sell takeaway food from their door, rather than only by delivery – which few of them have done. If Da Ivo opens its doors, who knows, I might enjoy a takeaway Buffalo Bill pizza next week.

I hope we can get meals from some of our favourite restaurants, as it will make a change after being locked down for eight weeks, and will give them badly needed custom. I'm very fond of Roman cuisine, as you'll have seen from the recipes I've included in this diary, and we cook a good deal of it at home. But now, as Rome's professional kitchens begin to stir back into life, this seems a good moment to ask, is Roman cuisine really that good?

One of the delights of Italy is that it's intensely local. It wasn't too long ago that Italy's regions were separate kingdoms and dukedoms, and if you drive for fifty or a hundred miles in any direction, people will speak a different dialect that even other Italians may struggle to understand. As well as the administrative boundaries that are marked clearly on maps, there are also invisible, ancient frontiers. One of the most curious of these lies between Rome and Naples. North of this line, if someone disagrees with you, they shake their head, as they do in Western Europe and the Americas. South of the line, people sharply lift their chin, as they do from Greece to India.

Italy is equally regional when it comes to food, and Tuscans, Neapolitans, Venetians, Bolognese, Milanese, Puglians, Sicilians, Torinese, Genoans and Sardinians all take great pride in their cuisine. Within this constellation, though, I wouldn't say that Rome is ranked particularly high. Romans will tell you that their dishes evolved from making something out of cheap off-cuts. The rich – high church-men, aristocrats and bankers – took the good meat and ordinary Romans developed a cuisine from what remained. Many Roman pasta dishes use *guanciale* – smoked fatty pork cheek – and our *portiera*, Cinzia, is always praising the virtue of tripe and urging me to try it, though I'm not tempted, however ingeniously it's prepared. Yet, even if it's not Italy's most sophisticated cuisine, I have to say that I'm very fond of Roman food. It has a way of robustly battling flavours against one another. An *amatriciana* sauce sets the sweetness of the tomato against the saltiness of the pecorino cheese. *Cacio e pepe* sets up the rich creaminess of the pecorino against the sharpness of the black pepper.

And Roman food has a secret weapon. When I was in my twenties, living in the UK, and was less interested in food than now, I'd sometimes make a simple pasta dish with onion, fresh tomatoes and tinned tuna – not exciting but it filled the stomach. One day, shortly after I came to live in Rome in the late 1980s, I made the same dish. I took a bite and wondered what on earth had happened. It tasted like an entirely different sauce, all thanks to the ingredients: the tomatoes and onions were a thing apart from the ones I was used to back in the UK. Tomatoes here are far sweeter and tangier, even compared to those from northern Italy, while the fruit and vegetables are as good as I've tasted in any country. Part of the reason will be the sun, but I suspect it's also down to a long history of unnatural selection. I've watched Roman matrons in the markets, berating marketeers over items that haven't met their high standards. Generations of demanding Romans have left their mark.

Rome, like all of Italy, is intensely food-focussed. If several Romans are gathered together talking, there's a good chance they'll be discussing food. If I'm at the market and I see something that I've never cooked, I sometimes ask the seller what should be done with it, and within moments other customers will usually join in, offering suggestions – and very good suggestions they generally are, too. At times it feels as if the whole population of Rome forms a very sophisticated recipe book.

If Italians have a weakness when it comes to food, it's their conservatism. There's a correct way to make an *amatriciana* sauce and any other approach is frowned upon, just as the sight of a foreigner ordering a cappuccino rather than an espresso café after lunch – which no Roman would do, as it's too heavy – will cause quiet dismay. The situation is much better than it used to be. When Shannon and I first moved here, eighteen years ago, it was hard to find anything but the classic, staple ingredients, and even fresh ginger or limes were difficult to buy. However, both are now available everywhere, and at the market by Piazza Vittorio one can find a rich selection of Indian and Far Eastern ingredients (though they won't impress anyone from London or New York).

As to restaurants, I'm happy to say that there are still plenty of excellent old-fashioned places with traditional decor that serve *carbonara* and the other favourites. Some of the best are in Testaccio, and I mentioned them during my account of the area, while one can find others dotted all around the city. Alongside these, though, there is now a new generation of hyper-fashionable places with eye-catching interiors and international influences in their menus. One of these is Madre, just off Via Nazionale. Built in a former convent, it's decorated with photographs of model-like girls wearing nuns' habits, smiling and standing in highly suggestive poses. The dining room is spectacular, with plants growing up the walls and hanging from the ceiling, while the food – which is good but not the best I've had in Rome – has a South American flavour.

Or there's Pianostrada. Run by several women, this began in a tiny, poky back alley of Trastevere, and as it only had a street-food licence, customers had to sit on high stools at tiny tables and use plastic cutlery. But the food was wonderful and it soon won a well-deserved rave review in the *New York Times*. Some of Pianostrada's inventions combine the foreign and the very Roman. They offer a burger made from that favourite Roman Friday-night staple, cod (the *baccaburger*) and another burger with crunchy pork cheek, caramelized onion and raschera cheese. Needless to say, they soon moved out of their first premises and now have a splendid, spacious place just across the Ponte Sisto bridge, and another to the south of here, with a spectacular roof terrace overlooking the river. And there are a lot of other superb non-traditional restaurants in Rome, many of which have opened fairly recently. To name a few: Vittorio Spezie e Cucina by Piazza Vittorio, Osteria Fratelli Mori by Via Ostiense, Zia in Trastevere and Osteria Fernanda in the Porta Portese area.

And yet, for the capital city of a large Western European country, I wouldn't say that Rome has much variety when it comes to food. There are a number of Chinese restaurants but most are old fashioned compared to what one can find in London or Paris, and the same is true of Indian food here, while I have yet to find a good Thai restaurant. Nor is the rest of Europe much represented. I know of no good French or Spanish place in Rome. Even the cuisine of most of Italy is absent. There are Sicilian and Neapolitan res-taurants but you'll struggle to enjoy a Tuscan or Venetian meal, let alone find a quality *Cotoletta alla Milanese* (veal cooked in breadcrumbs).

Fortunately, one can always drown one's sorrows with some ice cream. As with restaurants, Roman ice cream has a new/old split. For a magnificently old-fashioned gelato in the city centre there is Giolitti, close to the parliament buildings. Or, if you don't mind going a little farther afield, there's the equally legendary Palazzo del Freddo Giovanni Fassi by Piazza Vittorio, which was founded in 1880 and looks like it's hardly changed since the day it opened. For the new establishments there are numerous choices. Gelateria La Romana on the Viale Ostiense is a big, spectacular place with chocolate flowing from taps nonstop. Other smaller places offer highly novel flavours: Gelato Fantasia on the Viale Aventino sometimes has a brie and blueberry ice cream (much better than you'd think), at the tiny Gelateria Corona by Largo Argentina I've had celery and lime, and also white chocolate and red pepper – both excellent – while Fatamorgana, in our local square, Piazza San Cosimato, has a whole series of ice creams that use chocolate from different parts of the world, as well as a delicious passion fruit flavour.

When it comes to the award for Rome's best ice cream, though, there's no question: it goes to San Crispino. This gelateria began in an uninspiring residential street near San Giovanni, but then another branch was opened behind the Trevi Fountain, then a third near the Pantheon and there's now one at Fiumicino airport. San Crispino is a serious place. Until recently they offered no cones, only cups. The ice cream is not on view but is hidden away in storage pots set into the counter, with gleaming metal lids, where the temperature can be kept at exactly the correct level. Many of the flavours are simple, with just one ingredient, but they're perfect, with an abundance of flavour in every spoonful. My personal favourite is chocolate with meringue. Once, years ago, San Crispino offered aged balsamic vinegar ice cream and though it sounds vile, I have to say it was superb.

I'm confident the *gelaterie* will survive this storm. Many are compact in size, so their rents should be fairly low, and most of them have been going for a good while. Likewise, I'm hopeful for the old-fashioned Roman trattoria, all of which have been around for decades. I'm more nervous for the new and fashionable places. It would be a great shame if any are lost, as I have to say that I've never known Roman food to be as good as it is now. During the last year or two I have found a number of new restaurants where the food has been of outstanding quality and highly original.

We'll begin to see how they're all doing next week.

Wednesday the 29th of April

Rome: ideological showcase – and a recipe for *Pasta all'Amatriciana*

Yesterday I saw something wonderful on the web. A group of pilots who race drones freestyle, and who go by the name of Dirty Seagulls, have produced a video of deserted Rome as if seen through the eyes of a bird. It's a glorious piece of footage as a drone camera speeds low round the Fontana dei Quattro Fiumi (Fountain of the Four Rivers) in Piazza Navona, through the columns of the portico of the Pantheon, round the vast equestrian statue of Vittorio Emanuele on the huge marble monument of the Vittoriano, and rises vertiginously high above buildings, piazzas and obelisks. At one point you can hear the faint clang of a church bell in the distance.

Garibaldi famously remarked that Rome was a theatre, and it can sometimes feel like an immense set, waiting for the drama. It's hardly a surprise as, since its earliest days, Rome has always been a showpiece city. Its first great effort to make itself into a metropolis – draining and paving the Forum – was a practical change that created more space, uniting the hilltops and getting rid of a malarial swamp,

253

but it also permitted a display of power. The buildings erected in the Forum gave grandeur to Rome's politics, with a new Senate House and a royal palace, and also to its religion, with a temple to Vesta, where a team of dedicated virgins tended the perpetual fire that was believed to keep Rome safe.

A century and a half later, another great project was undertaken, when a new brick and timber temple was constructed on the Capitoline Hill, to Rome's chief god, Jupiter Optimus Maximus (Best and Greatest). It was probably the largest temple in the central Mediterranean and versions of it (the building burned down several times and was repeatedly rebuilt) would dominate Rome's skyline for a thousand years. But it proved very unlucky for the Roman king – Tarquin the Proud – who created it. The immense expense and labour required for its making were a major factor in his, and the monarchy's, fall.

Not many monuments survive from the five centuries of Rome's Republic, but one can get a sense of how it sought to display itself if you look down at the buildings unearthed in Largo Argentina, whose ruins are now used as a sunbathing area by cats from the adjoining sanctuary. In the republican era this low-lying area, which was intermittently flooded by the Tiber, lay outside the city walls and was used for military training and assembling Romans to vote. The Largo Argentina contains the usual palimpsest of ruins, including several Republican temples, which are thought to mark military victories. Rome at this time comes across as rather grim: a serious, functional city, fixated with war and filled with memorials to successful conquests and slaughters.

It was after the Republic fell that Rome truly became a display case of power. Over the course of five centuries, whole neighbourhoods of the city were demolished to make way for grand projects to show off imperial prestige. New building techniques using moulded concrete allowed immense buildings to be created, as emperors competed with their dead predecessors and put their names to new theatres and amphitheatres, new forums, new palaces and, above all, new baths. Though much from this time has been lost over the centuries, the dwarfing scale of imperial buildings can still be gauged from the ruins of the Baths of Caracalla and, even more so, from the Baths of Diocletian, remains of which are now spread across a museum, two churches and various smaller sites. As to what the baths looked like inside, decoration is well preserved in the church of Santa Maria degli Angeli e dei Martiri. Or you can drop into the Pantheon, where the walls display the look that would have appeared in numerous great buildings of this era, and which combined three kinds of coloured marble: green, a yellowy orange and a rich dark red. The last two are the colours of the city of Rome, and of Rome football club, to this day.

During the Roman Empire's final century and a half,

the emperors, now Christian, found a new way to show off: immense churches. Sadly, the two greatest of these are gone: the original Saint Peter's Basilica was demolished in the sixteenth century and San Paolo Fuori le Mura (Saint Paul's Outside the Walls), which had survived largely intact for fifteen centuries, burned down in 1823 (the papacy blamed the Jews but the real culprits were workmen repairing the roof).

Like the last of the emperors, Rome's medieval popes displayed their power through building churches, most of which are still standing, though these were on a smaller scale than earlier architectural efforts. Rome entered its greatest era of showing off during the Renaissance and Baroque ages. A new building spree was inspired by Catholicism's worst disaster: the Protestant Reformation. Popes hoped the catastrophe might be undone if they could dazzle obstinate Protestant heretics with a Rome remade as an ideological showpiece – a kind of Moscow Underground of its time. With the help of silver and gold looted from the Americas, the city was transformed: long-defunct classical aqueducts were repaired and flowed again, feeding elegant new fountains. New papal palaces rose up, and of course new churches. There were new roads with grand vistas of distant obelisks. Rome gained a new Saint Peter's Square, flanked by Bernini's immense curved colonnades, and a new Saint Peter's Basilica with an immense dome that dominated a new skyline of domes.

The project was a failure and the Protestant heretics were never brought back into the fold, but the city of Rome was much improved.

After 1870, when the popes were chased from the city to sulk in the Vatican, Rome became an anti-papal show-piece. The kings of Italy set up statues of all the figures most likely to irritate clerics, from the scientific thinker Giordano Bruno, whom the Church had burned at the stake, to Garibaldi. They also created a vast monster of a building that was intended to rival Saint Peter's Basilica: the marble Vittoriano, better known as the Wedding Cake, which com-memorated Italian unification. As to what Mussolini got up to trying to show off Fascism, that we've already seen. We can only be grateful his rule didn't last longer than it did, or he would have caused even more destruction. Since his fall, Romans have had enough of ideological showcasing and they've been happy to leave their city alone.

Yet, it's the combination of all these layers of display that make Rome the feast for the eyes that it is. Stand on the Gianicolo Hill, in front of Garibaldi glowering down from his horse, and before you lies two thousand years of rival architecture competing for your attention. You can make out the ancient stonework of the Colosseum, and of the Circo Massimo chariot-racing track. You can see the roof of the Pantheon, which from up here looks a little like a flying saucer. You can see medieval churches and bell towers, Renaissance and Baroque domes, including

Saint Peter's, and you can see the gleaming white bulk of the Vittoriano. Come here at dusk, as the last glow of the sun fades and the city lights come on, or on an autumn afternoon when the city lies beneath a stormy sky, and you really have a spectacle.

Rome after a November thunderstorm.

I can't claim Rome is dynamic. It's not hurried and productive like Milan or London, New York or Shanghai. It's not a good place to come if you want to shake the world with innovation. Its virtues are its food, its climate, its seasons, its light and its colours. And also its people who, in their selfishly cynical way, are warm and easy-going. All of these things are superficial, that I won't deny, but put them all together and they can be hard to resist.

As this entry has become a celebration of Rome, and as we haven't had a recipe for a while, I think I should end with that most Roman of dishes, *Pasta all'Amatriciana*. It's named after the town Amatrice, which lies in the Apennines not far from Rome and which was devastated in the terrible earthquake of August 2016. We visited the town years back and it was a beautiful little place. Soon after the earthquake we happened to take a cab in Rome. Roman cab drivers have a reputation for being tough and not always honest (though I've rarely found them tricky) but that day gave me a new view of the profession. The driver told us how, a few days earlier, an immense convoy of Roman cab drivers had set off to Amatrice with food and other supplies to give to the people who suddenly found themselves homeless.

Pasta all'Amatriciana

Serves four

Ingredients:

1 large onion, chopped.

Dry white wine – at least a cup

Pancetta, sweet not smoked – 4 thick pieces chopped into cubes (Romans use *guanciale* [smoked pork cheek] but bacon will do fine)

500g tomatoes – the sauce will be tastiest with fresh tomatoes (scald them in boiling water for a minute and then peel the skins), but it will taste fine with a passata of tomatoes or tinned plum tomatoes

1 red chilli pepper (according to taste)

500g pasta – Romans like to use a thick string called bucatini but if it's hard to find (and I should warn you, it's very messy to eat) a thick tube, like rigatoni or tortiglioni, is also fine

Pecorino Romano cheese – a good bowlful

Method:

Put the water for the pasta on to boil.

Cook the onion till soft and yellow, adding wine to stop it burning.

Add the pancetta and cook till a little crispy, again adding wine.

Add the tomato and chilli pepper. By now you can start cooking the pasta.

Cook the sauce until it's a good consistency and not too liquid.

When the pasta and sauce are ready, take the sauce off the heat and add a couple of tablespoons of pecorino to give it a rich creaminess.

Serve with more pecorino on the side.

Thursday the 30th of April

Is there a film that truly captures Rome?

Today, employees of the *Comune di Roma* have been strimming the green patch beneath our apartment, clearing the spring grass and other undergrowth. I was surprised. As it has been much neglected for some time, what with the financial crisis and the *Mafia Capitale* scandal, I'd assumed that, in lockdown, nothing would be done. The *Comune* seems to be functioning well in these coronavirus days, and rather better than it usually does. As far as I can judge by walks within our bubble, there's far less rubbish strewn about than there is usually. Before the lockdown, the rubbish collection people, AMA, never came often enough and the bins on our street regularly became surrounded by smelly bags, but now all is clean and tidy. I suppose a lot of our neighbours have left Rome, while those who remain are discarding less waste. I do hope that we learn something from this crisis, and that when it's over we don't step straight back to where we were. As to the strimming, in other years I'd be glad of it, as it eases my hay fever, but this time I feel rather sorry. The spring flowers are all gone and there'll be no more taking pictures of beetles.

Another piece of news is that *La Repubblica* ran a piece this morning on how the lockdown is affecting Circo Lidia Togni. This old Roman institution is based for much of the year on the Via Appia, in the direction of Ciampino Airport. The circus was just about to set out on a tour of Italy when Conte's first decree was unveiled and it found itself grounded in Rome. *La Repubblica* isn't averse to the lyrical and the report recounted how 'The big white and red tent is down, the human cannonball has said his farewells, gone are the children and also the ticket receipts, and now the only visitors are volunteers who bring a little cheer and also food'. The delivery of food was very necessary, as many circus employees had gone home and the twenty people who remained, half of them children, were unable to leave the circus area. They sought help from a group of volunteers who usually take necessities to the old and the needy. Now, three times a week these volunteers go to a bulk-buy supermarket and purchase meat for the tigers and dogs, and bring hay for the horse and llamas. As *La Repubblica* recounted, on their arrival at the circus grounds 'the dogs barked and wagged their tails, in the distance you could hear the squawking of the geese, and even the African oxen with their huge horns seemed excited'.

We once went to Lidia Togni's circus. That was more than a dozen years back and I'm sure it's changed since but, as happens quite often in Rome, my impression was of having suddenly stepped back a few decades. There was a female contortionist who, though she remained fully clothed, managed to display every part of her body to striking effect, and though there was nothing that would count as animal cruelty, there was a good deal of animal annoying. Still it was a great improvement on the world of wandering entertainers portrayed in Fellini's 1954 masterpiece, *La Strada* – a film in which brutality and indifference are shockingly present. We saw it just recently because, as I imagine much of the world has been doing, we've been warding off evening boredom by watching some classic films. Two of Fellini's greatest films were studies of Rome. So, we come to a question that I'd like to ask: has a film been made that truly captures the city?

Two of the most famous can quickly be discounted. *Roman Holiday* (1953) and *Three Coins in the Fountain* (1954) say more about post-war America than they do about Rome, which forms little more than a photogenic, romantic backdrop. (Woody Allen's *To Rome With Love*, from 2012, which must count as one of his weakest films, is no better.) Far better to look at that classic, *Ladri di biciclette* or *Bicycle Thieves* (1948), which is a wonderful proof that in cinema less can be more. With a cast that had no acting experience – the lead had been working in a factory – it tells the story, during the bleak days just after the war, of a father and son trying to retrieve a stolen bicycle, and yet it's one of the most powerful and heartbreaking films you're ever likely to see. It's also a wonderful portrait of the city at this unhappy moment, filled with finely observed details. It conveys the toughness of Romans and says much about where that toughness springs from. People here haven't forgotten those days when they, or their parents or grandparents, had to live by their wits.

The same harsh era is conveyed, in a very different way, in a comic film that's much less well known, at least outside Italy, *Guardie e ladri* (*Cops and Robbers*) from 1951. Oddly enough, the most unsympathetic character in the story is an American aid worker, overseeing food relief to hungry Romans. After being conned into buying a fake ancient coin, he insists the petty criminals who cheated him must be caught. The policeman charged with the case, who fears losing his job, goes undercover and introduces his family to the family of the chief suspect (played by one of Italy's greatest comic actors, Totò), only to find that a romance springs up between his daughter and the criminal's son. The film has a long chase scene which is utterly Roman. Beginning with two cars hurtling through city streets, it grows ever slower and ends with Totò, who was as thin as a stick, sitting on a country road, while the portly policeman leans on a haystack, wheezing for breath. Totò gestures with his hands to portray the other's stomach and holds up a finger to say, without words, what d'you expect, I'm thin and you're fat. The film ends with a fine example of odd Roman humanity, when Totò – the thief – leads the policeman by the hand and urges him to have courage and send him to jail.

It was a very different Rome that was revealed just nine years later, in the film that gave a name to its era: *La Dolce Vita* (1960). In it, Federico Fellini shows us a boomtown Rome: a city of ambition, of money to be made, of new apartment blocks springing up, and flash cafes on the Via Veneto. The film captures the delights of the city with some of the most gorgeous footage of Rome, notably the scene when, in the dead of night, Anita Ekberg wades into the Trevi Fountain. But it also has one of the most brutal depictions of self-serving Romans, when a group of freelance photographers (one of whom, Paparazzo, gave a name to the whole profession) can't be dissuaded from taking pictures of a woman who has yet to learn that her husband has killed himself and their children. The following year an even more brutal portrait of Rome appeared in Pier Paolo Pasolini's *Accattone* or *The Scrounger* (1961). Like *Bicycle Thieves*, it used no professional actors and it tells the story of a grasping lowlife who falls in love with a girl filled with goodness and innocence and turns her into a corrupted reprobate like himself.

A decade later Fellini produced another great film about the city: *Roma* (1972). If *La Dolce Vita* has a wandering storyline, *Roma* has no storyline at all, and consists wholly of episodes, veering between contemporary Rome and the city in the late Fascist era. Some sections, especially in the second half, are slow and far too long, but it captures the absurdity of Fascist Italy, the catastrophe of the war Mussolini led the country into, and the enduring consequences of that time. An extraordinary scene, in which a film crew is shown shooting the motorway approaches to Rome during a thunderstorm, ends with a traffic jam of cars gridlocked by the Colosseum, halted by a demonstration against, among other things, the mysterious neo-fascist Prince Borghese coup, that had been attempted only a few months before the film was made. And the film captures the theatre of Rome, especially in a scene that depicts a fantastical Catholic fashion show, in which models show off increasingly outlandish costumes on an immense curved catwalk.

Four decades later a film appeared that clearly looked over its shoulder to Fellini's great films but which brings Rome thoroughly up to date. Paolo Sorrentino's *La grande bellezza* or *The Great Beauty* (2013) is a visual feast from beginning to end, and offers a wonderful portrait of Rome at the end of the Berlusconi era, in which Romans are hungrily wedded to the shallow appearance of things. If the Rome it portrays isn't always one I recognize, that's probably because I don't move in the right circles. The protagonist, played with fine world-weariness by Toni Servillo, is a journalist, and our journalist friend, Barbie, found the scenes of lavish, hollow parties rang true to her. The film certainly captures the alluring, torpid listlessness of Rome, if in a romanticized way (you never see a traffic jam and the streets are cleaner than any Rome streets I've seen for a long time).

If I had to choose a film that truly captures the spirit of Rome, it's one that was made five years earlier, on a shoestring. In the tradition of *Bicycle Thieves* and *Accattone*, with the exception of the director, co-writer and lead, Gianni Di Gregorio, it used no professional actors. Barely a full-length film at only seventy-three minutes, *Pranzo di ferragosto* or *The Mid-August Lunch* (2008) tells the story of an indolent middle-aged Roman who lives with his ninety-something-year-old mother. In return for the cancellation of debts that he owes to the condominium of the apartment block where he lives, he's persuaded to look after the elderly mother of the condominium administrator who is escaping with his mistress during Rome's deadest summer holiday, Ferragosto. The administrator then rips him off and lands him with caring for a third old lady, too. I may be biased, as the film was made close to our home – some of it was filmed within our lockdown bubble and I often see the director in our neighbourhood – but I feel it perfectly captures the beauty, the melancholy, the humanity and the lassitude of Rome.

Saturday the 2nd of May

What do Romans think of their city's past?

Yesterday was May Day, one of Italy's biggest holidays. In Rome it's usually celebrated with a rock concert held by the Basilica of San Giovanni in Laterano but this year, naturally, all was online. Sting, who is very popular here, and was the biggest name in the concert, praised Italian health workers and then played, appropriately enough, 'Don't Stand So Close to Me'.

La Repubblica had photographs of Saint Peter's Square which, like other piazzas, now has a green fuzz of grass growing between the cobblestones, as there are no feet to tramp it down. The paper also had stories of how, despite government promises of financial help for those hit by the crisis, banks and bureaucrats are answering requests for help with procrastination. It doesn't surprise me. In my experience, Romans tend to be reluctant to part with money and late payments are a constant problem for small businesses. It's probably a legacy of centuries of tough times. On a brighter note, the authorities are giving out more details of plans to ease the lockdown on Monday – phase two. The metro is to be opened for the first time in weeks, with masks available for passengers. Bars and restaurants offering deliveries, along with parks and public transport, will all be subject to surveillance to make sure social distancing is maintained. I'm glad of it. The numbers of infected in Lazio have been slow to decrease and it would be a great shame if everybody's sacrifices were thrown away now, when they're finally having an effect.

Another piece of news is that, in these days of closed museums, the Ministry of Heritage and Cultural Activities for Tourism has put online a short video of the Pyramid of Cestius: the tomb of a first century BC Roman nobleman who chose to be buried in the style of a pharaoh. It's a place that I've always been curious to see inside. The video showed a chamber decorated with simple geometrical wall paintings. It looked interesting, but not *that* interesting, and I suspect I won't struggle too hard to see it in person. That's the trouble with spending your days living among extraordinary remains from the past: it's easy to grow lazy. There's so much to see here. In the last few years there's been more than ever, as the authorities have now opened many of the city's more obscure sites to reserved-place guided tours, which usually take place on weekends. I've been to one or two and they're well done, with knowledgeable guides. Though some foreigners join them, most are Romans, keen to see something new in their city.

Romans have always had a complex view of their monuments. From classical times onwards many Romans have been rightly proud of their city, and this pride even led them into early political activism. In the twelfth century, they rebelled against the unfettered power of the popes and created their own civic authority – a new senate, which met on the Capitoline Hill, where Rome's mayors still have their offices – and evidence suggests that they had been roused to action by papal looting of stone from the Baths of Caracalla, and plans to demolish Trajan's Column.

Yet many Romans, like many popes, saw their city first and foremost as a resource to be used. Even during Rome's glory days of empire, demolition and recycling were common. Statues of yesterday's men would routinely have their heads removed and replaced by those of the new generation. Matters became worse when Rome's fortunes failed. If marble is burned, it makes plaster, a useful commodity, and archaeologists have found remains of a series of ovens dating from the period when classical Rome entered its decline. As well as marble, ancient sites were quarried for stone, and the metal links that held stone blocks together were carefully removed (fine until an earthquake brought the whole thing down). It's no accident that much of what remains of classical Rome's monuments are fronted with bricks, as this was the one material that had no resale value – the stone and marble have largely vanished.

Those who were most sentimental about preserving the city's past were often foreigners rather than Romans. In the dark days of the early sixth century, the figure who was most concerned to conserve Rome's past was the barbarian Ostrogoth King Theodoric, who gave money and materials for the repair of the Baths of Caracalla, the athletic stadium on the Campus Martius (now the Piazza Navona) and even the pagan temple to Vesta in the Forum, which had been empty of its famous Vestal Virgins for more than a century.

The best friend of Rome's monuments was often catastrophe. In the truly disastrous days of the late sixth century there was no market even for recycled materials. Unable to build new churches, popes made do with converting old buildings – a need which saved the classical Senate House in the Forum and the Pantheon. Likewise, the greatest threat to Rome's monuments was a cash-rich pope eager to leave his mark. Destruction reached its peak during the Renaissance and Baroque eras when, as Spanish silver flowed into the city from the Americas, numerous ancient buildings quietly disappeared and were used to rebuild Rome as a Counter-Reformation showpiece. The stones of the southern, outer wall of the Colosseum, which had collapsed of its own accord, make up a good part of the fabric of Saint Peter's Basilica.

By the nineteenth century popes were finally showing an interest in preserving Rome's pagan heritage. Some monuments, including the Colosseum, were strengthened, though looting continued, and much was lost during the frenzy of construction that came when Rome became the capital of a newly unified Italy in 1870. Even recently I've heard talk of building contractors who fail to report findings of ancient remains and simply destroy them for fear of interminable delays. Not all Romans would condemn them for their actions. I've met people here who find the city's past exasperating, and who complain, 'Monuments? What can you do with monuments?' The city's immense history can leave them with a sense of futility – how can you hope to leave any trace of yourself when you walk in the footsteps of Cicero, Julius Caesar, Raphael, Michelangelo and so many others? The last Roman resident who tried to shake up the world was Mussolini, and that didn't end well. For some Romans, having been brought up among so many relics of history has left them with a dislike of the past and a hunger for the modern, and they dream of living in Tokyo or Berlin or Shanghai, where everything is new and efficient. When Shannon goes to visit her family, the cab drivers who take her to the airport often regale her with their enthusiasm for Canada, believing it to be a land where everything works and anything is possible (though in Canada she often has the same experience in reverse, and is told how lucky she is to live in Rome, where everything's so beautiful and old).

Many of Rome's greatest devotees are foreigners. Titus Livius – better known as Livy – the writer of a truly monumental history of Rome in the first century BC, in 142 volumes, was from Padua, then very much foreign territory. Ferdinand Gregorovius, the author of another vast history of the city, this time covering the Middle Ages, was from a city in East Prussia, now Poland. Richard Krautheimer, who was the greatest authority on Rome's architectural history, was from Germany and then fled the Nazis to the USA.

Yet, if foreigners include some of the most knowledgeable writers on Rome, there is one aspect of the city's past that only Romans can grasp. When I taught English here in the late 1980s I had a student who was very mature indeed: a grandmother in her eighties. She told me about her childhood growing up in the Fascist era when, most of all, she remembered the tedium of endless obligatory political meetings. During the German occupation she joined the Roman Resistance. She and others went to Saint Peter's Square when the pope made an appearance on the balcony, where they hurled out leaflets, knowing they'd probably be safe from arrest amid the huge crowds.

All these experiences left her firmly on the left when it came to politics, even when it came to the distant past. We once came to discussing Cicero, the politician, orator and defender of the Roman Republic, and how he had crushed a plot by the aristocratic revolutionary, Catiline. The event is well recorded, thanks to the survival of Cicero's speeches, and my understanding of it – provided by my A-level in ancient history – was that Cicero had been a pompous but decent man acting as best he could at a dangerous moment. My student, though, had a very different view. 'Cicero was a bastard,' she told me, with feeling. 'Catiline was a man of the people.' She had lined up first-century BC Roman politics with those of her own time. In her eyes Cicero was a Christian Democrat stooge of a corrupt, self-serving establishment and Catiline was a hero of the left. For her, Rome's past was not a wonderful conundrum to be studied and understood, but a world she was still living in, for better and worse.

Was there a golden age of Rome?

Today is the last day before the easing of the lockdown. I feel excited, certainly, but also a little anxious. The French philosopher, Jean-Jacques Rousseau, famously wrote, 'There's tranquillity in dungeons, but is that enough to make them desirable?' Certainly not, and yet you do get used to them after a time – and the lack of blaring car horns has made a nice change.

Besides, it's not as if the crisis is anywhere near over. Our region of Lazio, in particular, is struggling, and though the number infected here is far lower than it is in the north, the authorities are having trouble getting the situation fully under control. In the last couple of days two new clusters of cases have emerged. Yesterday, twenty-two new infections were announced in an old people's home in the San Giovanni area, and there have been no fewer than sixty-five at the Catholic Salesian Pontifical University just north of the city. The president of the Rome medical association, Antonio Magi, warned today that too many Romans are out and about, driving or gathering on foot outside supermarkets and shops. 'We're balanced on the edge of a cliff,'

Magi said. 'It won't take much to lose everything that we've gained.'

In the meantime, the Italian authorities have further clarified what will be possible from tomorrow, though I can see some problems with the policing of the rules. We won't be allowed to visit friends, though with masks and social distancing we'll be permitted to get together with our spouses, our live-in partners (whom you'd think we'd be with already), along with partners of civil unions, and those with whom we have stable emotional ties. As to family, we're allowed to spend time with blood relatives several times removed, including our cousins' children, but we're not permitted to see the children of the cousins of our spouse. I can see the police calling out from a half rolled-down window, 'So is this the daughter of your cousin by blood or by your wife's cousin?' Or, 'And this relationship of yours, you're quite sure it's truly stable emotionally?'

Best to be optimistic. In the past I've written a good deal about Rome's most desperate moments, when it was sacked by invaders. Now, to mark the last day of being locked down in our bubble, I'd like to look at Rome's best times and ask, was there a golden age of Rome?

One possible candidate for such a claim is more than two thousand years ago, when Rome was at a high point of confidence in the late 140s BC. The city had crushed its greatest rivals, Carthage and Macedonia, and was emerging as the superpower of the Western world. It was growing into the greatest city of the Mediterranean, with new aqueducts to bring fresh water to the population, and streets paved with volcanic stone from the Alban Hills. This was also a moment of cultural excitement. Greek writing and art were capturing minds and, for the first time, educated Romans were expected to be bilingual in Greek. In part thanks to Greek influence, Latin was becoming a language of literature. Some of Rome's great families were patrons of the arts, including the Scipios, who gave support to Gaius Lucilius, who is regarded as the father of the one literary form Rome gave to the world: satire.

Of course, even during the best of times, some things grow worse. Rome in the 140s BC was well on the way to becoming a slave state, where the free used and brutalized the unfree. The gap between the rich and poor was growing ever wider, and the wealthy were unwittingly destroying the heart of their state, as middling farmers lost their land to huge slave-run estates. However confident Rome was at this moment, I doubt modern eyes would find it a very likeable city. As we've seen, it was highly militaristic, filled with temples and triumphal arches commemorating victories, while, in spite of the elite's interest in Greek culture, Romans were highly suspicious of anything foreign, and Eastern religions were intermittently banned. Rome was dominated by handful of immensely rich families and though there was free speech it was as well to have powerful friends. Social upheavals lay just around the corner and the ultimate victors would be vastly wealthy individuals who, posing as defenders of the poor, would destroy constitutional government and install themselves as autocrats – the emperors.

The emperors had been ruling Rome for more than a century and a half by the time of my next proposed golden age, in the AD 150s. This was the era of one of Rome's dullest emperors, Antoninus Pius, who ruled during a decade when the Roman Empire, which now stretched from Scotland to Sudan and from Morocco to the Caspian Sea, was at peace, with hardly a single rebellion or barbarian attack. The city of Rome was at its height, with an estimated 1.5 million inhabitants, and its finest classical buildings had been constructed, from the Pantheon to the vast shopping mall and cultural centre of Trajan's Forum and Market. In terms of culture, Rome was a relatively arid place, as generations of dictatorship had gradually throttled creative thought, but its wealthier inhabitants lived comfortably. They were supplied with fresh water from eleven aqueducts, foods and luxuries from all across the empire, and an extensive supply of slaves and exotic animals that they could watch being slaughtered in the amphitheatre.

It wouldn't be long before this era would be remembered as a lucky time. During the 160s and 170s the empire erupted into violence, as enemies broke across its frontiers. It was also assaulted from within and for fifteen years it was devastated by successive waves of an epidemic, which appears to have originated in China, and is known as the Antonine Plague. Studies of symptoms suggest it was probably smallpox. It brought havoc to cities, armies and contributed to the Roman Empire's long and slow decline, which began at this time.

I'm not sure if my next choice, the era of Pope Gregory I, can count as a golden age, and I very much doubt anyone saw it as such at the time, but at least it was better than what had come before. The sixth century was a disastrous time for Rome, during which it was subjected to repeated sieges and sackings. The city was also devastated by Bubonic Plague and for a few weeks in 547 it was wholly abandoned. When Gregory became pope in 590, Rome was menaced by Italy's latest invaders, the Langobards, its buildings were in ruins, the Tiber was filled with snakes and dead cattle, and people were dying by the score from hunger and disease. Though the city was still in a poor state on his death, fourteen years later, life was a little less uncertain for the Romans. Gregory made peace with the Langobards, organized food supplies for the city from Church estates and gave the papacy new prestige by asserting its authority over churchmen in France and Spain. He even found time to send out a mission to convert some pagan barbarians who had been wreaking havoc on a distant, rainswept island: the English. The mission was a great success and changed British history.

If Gregory's reign wasn't a high point for Rome, it was for the papacy, which afterwards descended into an increasingly degraded institution, fought over by powerful families for its wealth. A nadir was reached in the late ninth century, when Pope Stephen VI organized a show trial of the corpse of his disinterred predecessor, Pope Formosus. Formosus' remains were dressed in full papal regalia, propped up on a chair and, when they failed to deny that they had gained office illegally, three rotting fingers were lopped off from their right (benediction) hand and the rest of the body was thrown into the Tiber. Pope Stephen's triumph was short-lived and he was deposed and strangled soon afterwards.

My next golden age is more clear-cut: the era of Pope Innocent III, who reigned from 1198 to 1216. At this time the papacy was as powerful as any of Europe's monarchies and Innocent's word could make and break kings. Rome was thriving. It was filled with fortress towers, bell towers and magnificent new churches decorated by the great artists of this era: Cavallini, Torriti and Rusuti. Innocent himself did little in the way of church building and his legacy was more practical. He created a new fortress on the Vatican Hill, from which today's immense Vatican Palace would eventually grow. He also built the most fearsome fortified tower in Rome, the Tor de' Conti, which still stands, bunker-like and threatening, close to the Forum. Yet if Innocent was good for Rome, it's doubtful that he was good for the rest of Europe. The crusaders he sent east to recapture Jerusalem changed their plans and sacked

Constantinople instead, a blow from which the Byzantine Empire never recovered. The decisions of the 1215 Vatican Council, which he oversaw, marked a new intolerance for Jews and any others whose views challenged the Church.

My next candidate is the first decades of the sixteenth century, at the height of the Renaissance. At this time the city was still very medieval in terms of comforts – it was overcrowded, it stank and as the ancient aqueducts barely functioned, Romans were reduced to drinking Tiber water – yet it had an undeniable charm. The popes were able to coax quantities of gold into their coffers and Italy's greatest artists came to the city, including Bramante, Michelangelo and the sculptor and writer of a famously self-aggrandizing autobiography, Benvenuto Cellini. It was a time when even popes could be highly knowledgeable about Rome's classical past, and when humanist writers gathered in gardens to drink, dine, compare antiquities they had found, and to read out their writings in fine Latin prose. Certainly, it was a moment that was remembered with sad nostalgia after it came to a sudden and horrific end with the 1527 sacking of the city, in which thousands of Romans were tortured, murdered and died of the plague.

I'm not sure my next proposal would have been thought of as a golden age by many Romans. During the 1830s and 40s Rome was governed by hyper-reactionary popes who filled jails with political prisoners, banned dancing the waltz, and subjected the city to a kind of moral thought police, who hunted out unmarried couples. Yet this was a delightful time for the hordes of northern Europeans and Americans who came to visit, for a holiday, for a winter season, and sometimes to live for decades. For them the papacy's strange way of ruling was quaint rather than oppressive. The city was now a small gem of Renaissance and Baroque fountains, palaces, domes, parks and city vistas. For artists, writers and rich people with time on their hands, Rome was a home from home, where they could find English stables, an English club, English tailors, shoemakers, dressmakers, saddlers, hairdressers, boot-makers and wine sellers. Many left in 1849 when the city became a battlefield between nationalist Roman revolu-tionaries and a French army sent to crush them, and the city really lost its charm to expats when the nationalists finally won and Rome, as capital of the newly unified Italy, became a building site.

Finally, I offer up the late 1950s and 1960s, that were christened by Fellini's cinematic masterpiece as the Dolce Vita years. This was the Rome I first saw, aged eight, in 1969. It was a time of excitement after the misery that fol-lowed the war. It was the era of Cinecittà, when Hollywood and Italian stars could be spotted sitting at cafes on the Via Veneto (my father pointed out Orson Welles to us, glumly eating breakfast at the hotel where we were staying, though I'm sorry to say that I was too young to know who he was). Of course, no time is without failings. A few years back I talked to an American couple who'd lived in Rome at the time, and when I remarked that it must have been extraordinary, they answered, 'It was, if you didn't mind tear gas.' This was also a time of great anger and political protest.

The trouble with any golden age is that, to quote Joni Mitchell, we don't know what we've got till it's gone. Who can say – in spite of the intermittent piles of rubbish on our street, the recession and the political worries, the last two decades may have been a golden age. I rather hope not. I'd hate to think this book could become a portrait of a glorious Rome lost, or that the virus will have helped overcome Romans' resistance to the modern, globalized world, and that their very personal way of doing things – the family-run restaurants and shops, the shouted first names on the street – will wither away.

I'm optimistic. I can't see Romans stopping being Romans. Their way of being runs very deep. My hope is that Rome's greatest golden age is yet to come.

Unlocked – and a recipe for *Pasta fredda*

Today was our liberation day, at least up to a point. Tatiana had online classes and so had to stay at home but the three remaining members of the family put on our masks and gloves, said our good mornings to Cinzia and set out. What kind of Rome was waiting for us? It was livelier, certainly. There were more people walking and the roads were busier than they have been since the lockdown began, though not busy enough to threaten a traffic jam.

We had some good surprises. The French bakery, Le Levain, was open for business, and a delighted Alexander had a cinnamon roll for breakfast. Better still, after seven weeks of closure, Roberto and Anna's delicatessen had reopened. There was a long queue, which was no surprise, and as we had no urgent need to go in, as we still have some of his pecorino and parmesan left, we simply said our hellos through the door and he and Anna waved very cheerfully. When Alexander checked on his phone, he found that Da Ivo has also reopened with a delivery service. Tonight, we'll have Buffalo Bill and Del Vecchio pizzas at home.

We passed the local market, said our hellos to Bruno, Sara and Matteo and then the great moment came: we stepped out of our ex-bubble and walked into the tourist square, Santa Maria in Trastevere, and then beyond, to the river, where we crossed the Ponte Sisto into a Rome that I hadn't seen for almost two months. It was a beautiful day, not a cloud in the sky, warm but not hot. Here we were in a land that had been unreachable for so long, and that I'd dreamed of seeing for weeks, yet I have to say, it seemed like something of an anticlimax. I'd been expecting a moment of relief and joy, and instead it felt quite ordinary. But then of course it did, as that was the whole idea. We had taken a small step back towards the everyday.

There were some who were very pleased to see us. We stopped at another bakery, which has a kind of heavy bread that Tatiana likes, and as Alexander and I waited across the road, I noticed a pigeon that was curiously fearless, and kept beetling about by our feet. I wondered if it was hungry. Alexander still hadn't finished his cinnamon roll so he took a bite, let a few crumbs fall to the ground and surely enough, the pigeon hurried to peck them up, and it was quickly joined by several others. They'll have sorely missed the crumbs that are normally dropped from innumerable pizzas and panini by tourists. And they'll have missed the pigeon woman, too, who I've seen going round the centre for years. She arrives with a bicycle, not riding but walking, which is a wise precaution as the pigeons all know her, and the moment she appears they fly over in a wave, crowding onto the carrier of her bike, where she keeps the bread. As they flap all around her, she flings it out, causing a frenzy. I doubt she's been here for the last couple of months.

We went to the Piazza Navona. After hearing Barbie's accounts, I'd imagined it would look almost like a field waving with weeds, but no, there was just a tiny fuzz of green shoots among the cobblestones. It was almost deserted and the Corso, which is full of clothes' shops, was the same. Near-empty buses rumbled past with signs in the windows announcing that all passengers had to wear masks. The Via Condotti, with its shuttered fashion shops for wealthy tourists, we had almost to ourselves. The same was true of Piazza di Spagna, where I saw there was not a soul on the Spanish Steps. At the Trevi Fountain, which is normally a pickpocket's paradise, crammed with tourists, there was nobody aside from a little group of police, chatting to one another.

By the Pantheon we found that one of Rome's most famous coffee bars, the Tazza d'Oro, was open for business, and for the first time since the lockdown began, we had a coffee away from our home. The process was a little convoluted. We had to place our order at a small table outside the entrance, paying at arm's length, then one of us only was allowed inside to collect the coffee, which was served in takeaway cups. When I emerged, Shannon was waiting with her phone to capture the moment with a photo and we were then stopped by a couple of freelance paparazzi, who took a series of pictures of us holding up our cups. Who knows, we might be in one of the papers tomorrow.

It was busier when we got back to Trastevere. Were people keeping themselves at a proper social distance? It was hard to tell. Some were close to one another but they could have been families just like us. We'll know better when the infection rates are announced in a week or two. From now on the numbers are likely to be misleading and it will be like reading good news in old newspapers, telling us of the last successes of the lockdown, when what's actually happening may be quite different.

Now I'm home, feeling tired but very content after our long walk. This liberty certainly broadens one's horizons. Tomorrow I think I might just go abroad, leave the Republic of Italy and burst across the frontier, into the Vatican City State. I'll go and see if the weeds in Saint Peter's Square are any higher than they are in Piazza Navona.

All in all, things could have been a great deal worse, and Rome has got off lightly, at least so far. In Lombardy there have been 78,000 cases and 14,000 deaths, while in Lazio, which contains Rome, Italy's largest city, there have been a tenth as many cases and twenty-seven times fewer deaths. The health system was never overwhelmed here. I read this morning that during the last two months the mortality rate in Rome has actually been 10 per cent *lower* than it usually is at this time of year. I can only imagine that numbers are down because there are no tourists dying here. Or that Romans have been preserved by the absence of pollution in the air, and because they haven't been able to crash into one another on the roads.

Looking back at the curve of infection, I see that the most dangerous moment was, unsurprisingly, just before the lockdown came into force, as it was about ten days later that new cases spiked. I was right to worry about my evening at the Oasis of Beer. I have no doubt at all that the government's decisive action, shutting down not just the worst affected areas in the north but the whole country, has saved a great number of Roman lives, one of which could be my own.

Who knows how the next months will go? Even if the numbers creep up, I'm hopeful the virus will remain contained until a vaccine can be found. I rather assume the world will then return to its old ways, though I do hope that something will be gained from this strange moment. It would be a great shame if, after all the pain that people have suffered, something good can't be learned from what's happened, and from the changes we've found we can make to our lives. Do we really need to fly and drive as much as we have done, filling the air with pollution? Do we need to constantly buy so many things?

There's something else that I'm glad of, along with not having come down with the virus. After all these years, during which I've read and written about Rome's long and remarkable history, there's now a little corner of it that I've lived myself, among the Romans.

Already the spring is passing. The blossom on the trees is fading and the leaves are turning dark green. In celebration of the end of the lockdown, and the end of this book, I'd like to give you a final recipe, one that's right for the coming season. It's *pasta fredda*, or cold pasta, which may not sound very tempting, but it's perfect on a sweltering hot evening. It could hardly be simpler and you can add almost anything you feel like, as it works with tuna, green beans and courgettes among other things. The only trick to it is to make sure the pasta is thoroughly cooled before you add the other ingredients. You can add parmesan cheese but you may find it's better without.

Pasta fredda

Serves four

Ingredients:

400g tomatoes – it's good with a mixture, some big meaty ones, some small Datterini or cherry tomatoes, and all as flavoursome as possible

2 tablespoons olive oil

250g mozzarella – the best possible, fior di latte is fine, bufala even better

250g black olives – tinned, de-stoned ones can work if you don't want to deal with the pips

Half a jar of pesto

500g farfalle pasta (penne rigate tubes will also do)

Basil – a good handful, shredded, but keep some back unshredded

Method:

Put on water for the pasta and while it's heating, chop the tomatoes, put them in a bowl, add the oil and all the other ingredients except the unshredded basil. Stir and leave at room temperature – however hot that may be – to sit.

Cook the pasta al dente. Rinse briefly under cold water till you're sure it's at room temperature.

Mix all together in bowl. Put the unshredded basil on top for decoration. Eat!

Acknowledgements

I would like to give all my thanks to our Roman friends, Renata Moro and Alessandra Grego, for their invaluable help with this manuscript, spotting errors and correcting my poor Italian.

My thanks also to Laura McCullagh, Philippa Perry, my sister Tacy, Colin Beagley, Stephen Greenblatt, Jhumpa Lahiri, Ben Preston, Donald Sturrock, Andrew Slaughter, Mary Hill, Ana Paula Lloyd and everybody who gave encouragement when first I sent out the emails that eventually grew into this book. Thanks, as ever, to my agent, Georgia Garrett, and also Will Atkinson and James Nightingale at Atlantic Books.

Most of all, thanks to my family for being such wonderful lockdown companions.

A Note About the Author

Matthew Kneale is the author of seven novels and three works of non-fiction. His debut novel, *Whore Banquets*, won the Somerset Maugham Award, *Sweet Thames* was awarded the John Llewellyn Rhys Prize and *English Passengers* was shortlisted for both the Man Booker Prize and the Miles Franklin Award, and won the Whitbread Book of the Year Award. His previous non-fiction book, *Rome: A History in Seven Sackings*, was a *Sunday Times* bestseller. He lives in Rome with his wife and two children.